Training Manual

Corporate Turnaround And Transformation Methodology

Published in 2007 by
Corporate Turnaround Centre Pte Ltd.

Printed in Singapore
by Markono Print Media Pte Ltd.

9 8 7 6 5 4
09   08

Training Manual

Corporate Turnaround
And Transformation
Methodology

2007 © Corporate Turnaround Center.

Document:	TM-CT 3.0
Author:	Dr Michael Teng, Corporate Turnaround Centre
Status:	Final
Last Modified on:	24 April 2009

Table of Contents

Author Background

Dr Mike Teng is the author of the book "*Corporate Turnaround: Nursing a sick company back to health*", in 2002 which is also translated into the Bahasa Indonesia. It was one of the top selling management books then. In 2006, he authored another book entitled, "*Corporate Wellness: 101 Principles in Turnaround and Transformation.*"

He has been interviewed on the national media on many occasions on the subject of corporate turnaround and transformation. Dr Teng is widely recognized as a turnaround CEO in Asia by the news media such as the Channel NewsAsia, News Radio FM 93.8, the Boss Magazine, Economic Bulletin, the Today, World Executive Digest, Lianhe ZaoPao, StarBiz and the Straits Times.

He has 27 years of experience in corporate turnaround, strategic planning and operational management responsibilities in the Asia Pacific region. Of these, he held Chief Executive Officer's positions for 17 years in multi-national, local and publicly listed companies. He led in the successful turnaround of several troubled companies.

Dr Teng served as the Executive Council member for fourteen years and the last four years as the President of the Marketing Institute of Singapore (2000 - 2004), the national body representing some 5000 individual and corporate members in Singapore. Dr Teng holds a Doctor in Business Administration (DBA) from the University of South Australia, Master in Business Administration (MBA) and Bachelor in Mechanical Engineering (BEng) from the National University of Singapore. He is also a Professional Engineer (P Eng, Singapore), Chartered Engineer (C Eng, UK) and Fellow Member of Chartered Institute of Marketing (FCIM), Chartered Management Institute (FCMI), Institute of Mechanical Engineers (FIMechE), Institute of Electrical Engineers (FIEE) and Senior Member of Singapore Computer Society (SMSCS).

Some Reviews of the work done by Dr. Mike Teng

Book reviews

Productivity Digest, May 2003, "Dr Teng shared his thoughts on Corporate Turnaround with some 120 chief executive officers (CEOs) and senior executives at a CEO Breakfast Talk."

STAR, 5 May 2003, "Overall, the book reads well with the help of many tables and illustrations. The currency and variety of the case studies provide another reading pleasure."

Australian Alumni Singapore Newsletter, April 2003, "Having served as a CEO of several troubled companies, Dr Teng had demonstrated his corporate turnaround skills by successfully rescuing them out of near financial stability and robust growth again. His unique approach of using medical analogies to drive home the concepts and methods of effective corporate turnaround presents businesses with turnaround solutions that are easy to grasp."

Silver Kris, March 2003, "Written by one of Asia's leading turnaround CEOs, Dr Michael Teng, Corporate Turnaround is aimed at companies experiencing a slump in business and facing no prospect of improvement in the foreseeable future."

Smart Investor, December 2002, "With a liberal helping of Sun Tzu and nods to Confucius and the Bible, Corporate Turnaround offers plenty of the author's own insights, not to mention pertinent examples drawn from the experiences of well-known companies that have managed to swim rather than sink."

Today, 29 July 2002, "Company sick? Call Dr Teng."

Peak Magazine, "In his new book, Corporate Turnaround, marketing maestro, Dr Mike Teng, dispenses his prescription for ailing Asian companies seeking relief from the economic doldrums."

Television and radio interview with the turnaround CEO, author and expert

Television

Channel NewsAsia television (45 minute programme in Strategic Mind, July 2003) interview with the author, "Widely known as the turnaround CEO in Asia."

NewsAsia television (5 minute programme in Singapore Business Tonight, December 2002), Interview with the author

Radio

News Radio 93.8 FM Positive Business Minutes, May 2004, September 2003, June 2002,
Words of wisdom on Corporate Turnaround by the author.

News Radio 93.8 FM Living Room, October 2002, "He is recognised as the turnaround CEO in Asia, the man who turned red into black, a local hero, CEO who led the companies under his purview to be the first to achieve ISO 9001 in their respective industry."

Other interviews and write-ups by the author

English

The Edge, 13 November 2005, "We're coming back, Informatics' deep, cost-cutting moves were necessary."
Business Times, 24, October 2004, "Informatics restructuring picks up speed."
The Straits Times, 26, June 2004, "New chief will bank on experience to lead Informatics."
Singapore Marketer, May 2004, Tribute to the author
The AlumNUS, April 2003, Article by the author
The AlumNUS, January 2003, Article by the author
Today, 3 November 2001, Article by the author,
The Business Times, 2 November 2001, Article by the author
Marketing, June 2002, Interview of the author
Economic Bulletin, August 1998, Article by the author,
World Executive Digest, October 1997, Interview of the author
Marketing News, March/April 1996, Article by the author
The Straits Times, 16 March 1996, "Men who turn red into black."

Mandarin

Lianhe Zaobao, 28 September 2005, "Informatics to attract more overseas students."
Lianhe Zaobao, 24 June 2004, "Dr Teng joining Informatics."
Lianhe Zaobao, 25 October 2003, Interview of the author
BlueSky Management, 9 March 2003, Article by the author
World Executive Digest, August 1998, Interview of the author
Boss Magazine, February 1998, Article by the author
Boss Magazine, January 1998, Article by the author
Boss Magazine, December 1997, Article by the author,

Section 1

Introduction

1. Introduction to the Training Manual

Introduction

Until a few years ago, turnaround specialists were a relatively unknown breed in the business world. However, as once-stable companies struggle to maintain profitability, the expertise of corporate renewal professionals is more in demand than ever. Rising competition, cyclical financial markets and economic volatility have created a climate where no business can take economic stability for granted.

Many companies have, in the past, turned to downsizing to improve their economic health. However, downsizing has taken its toll on corporations by robbing them of management talents. The ranks of managers groomed to assume top positions have been thinned. In addition, the volatile business environment has turned once-successful CEOs into hesitant managers who are no longer able to provide strong leadership.

It is with this background that the Course on Corporate Turnaround takes the audience through the processes of identifying the symptoms of corporate illness and then devising the right set of treatment to nurse the company back to health. This Manual is intended as a document that the participants of this course can refer to both during the course itself, and at any time later in their careers, as they put these concepts into practice.

Objectives of the Training Manual

At the end of the course, it is expected that the participants should be able to diagnose any potential case of corporate illness, and devise a well-defined set of steps that need to be undertaken to treat the entity and bring it back to better health in the short run as well as in the long run. In this context, this Training Manual is designed to help the participants through these learning outcomes.

The specific objectives of this Training Manual are:
 a) To provide supplementary material to reinforce what has been learnt during the course
 b) To highlight the salient concepts and methodologies taught, and
 c) To act as a Reference document for any future help required by the participants

Description of the Training Manual

The course on Corporate Turnaround itself relies extensively on the Medical Analogy espoused by the author. This Training Manual adopts a logical and user-friendly approach in bringing out the processes involved in Corporate Turnaround. It draws upon the contents and situations presented during the course, and portrays them in a style that facilitates easy recall.

Sections and modules are arranged in a logical order, which allows the participants to:

- first **understand what is Corporate illness**, and what are its typical symptoms
- then **define the role of each of the three phases of treatment**, Surgery, Resuscitation, and Nursing
- then **plan and execute the steps involved in each phase**, and implement them within the context of the organization

Besides providing the base material for learning and reference, the Manual includes Illustration Capsules at the end of each Section giving several real-life cases and examples to illustrate the points covered.

At the end of the Manual, two Case studies are included, which bring out some typical problems faced by turnaround managers, and bring out very vividly the processes involved in carrying out successful turnarounds.

Section 2

Corporate Illness

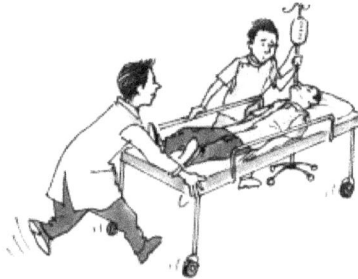

Physical and Fiscal Health

2. Corporate Illness

The Twenty-first century brings fresh challenges to many companies in Asia and around the world. As these companies venture into the new era, many will fail as they are unable to cope with the rapid pace of changes in the turbulent business environment. This inability may be due to antiquated strategies, obsolete products, poor management, corporate arrogance and many other factors. New challenges surface each day. Conventional wisdom and business practices that worked in the past may not work in the future and companies are thrown into a state of disarray and chaos. Past successes will not guarantee future successes.

The Asian economic miracle was invincible in the 1990s and would have heralded the 21st century as the Asian century. Unfortunately, this promising scenario ended abruptly in 1997. The economic crisis which started in Thailand quickly escalated and triggered massive capital outflows from Malaysia, Indonesia, South Korea and other parts of Southeast Asia. Eventually, these sudden events precipitated in the Asian currency meltdown. Barely following the economic crisis of 1997, many companies in Asia were being overwhelmed by macro factors such as worldwide recession brought forth by the economic recessions in the United States and Japan as well as political turmoil and regional economic malaise. The terrorist attacks on the United States on 11 September 2001 dealt severe blows to its economy as well as those in the Asia-Pacific region. Others are swept off their feet by micro factors such as market liberalization, proliferation of mergers and acquisitions, emergence of China as a formidable competitor, escalating costs and a host of other factors.

Most of these factors have led to some form of "Corporate Illness" or "Turnaround situations". It is difficult to define in indisputable terms as to what constitutes Corporate Illness, as it depends on the nature of sickness, socio-cultural differences, and the type of business (Service or Manufacturing). For the purpose of this Manual, **the term will be used to cover companies whose financial performance is doomed for failure in the foreseeable future if appropriate and timely corrective actions are not taken in both the short and long term.**

Normally, the word "turnaround" conjures up situations where the companies are plagued with immediate cash and/or profit crisis. However, the turnaround definition adopted here is wider and also encompasses companies that are not immediately affected by such crisis situations. This broad definition of a turnaround situation recognizes that companies often display **"telling" signs or symptoms of failure way before any crisis sets in, similar to a sick person initially showing signs of mild fever or tiredness.**

Common Symptoms

Most common symptoms of sick companies:

- ➤ Incompetent management
- ➤ Declining sales
- ➤ Low or negative profitability
- ➤ High Accounts Receivables
- ➤ Poor Inventory Turnover
- ➤ Unfavorable Leverage ratio
- ➤ High staff turnover

With any of these symptoms, Turnaround strategies must be adopted immediately to avoid further deterioration

Prevention is better than Cure

Medical Analogy

MEDICAL ANALOGY – I

HUMAN BEING	THE COMPANY
Marriage	Merger and acquisition
Pregnancy	Concept/ Idea
Baby	Start-up Company
Healthy	Good profitability and cash flow
Patient	Troubled Company
Sickness/ Ailment/ Disease	Trouble / Problem
Lifeblood	Cash flow
Hemorrhage	Loss of key staff
Tumors/ Cancers	Dysfunctional Employees
Doctor	Turnaround CEO/ Manager
Hospital	Bank/ Private Investor/ Venture Capitalist

"AN ANNUAL CORPORATE HEALTH CHECK IS FUNDAMENTAL."

MEDICAL ANALOGY – II

HUMAN BEING	THE COMPANY
Surgery	Restructuring/ Rationalising/ Downsizing/ Re-engineering
Resuscitation	Revitalisation of the sales and profits
Nursing/ Rehabilitating	Sustaining/ Nurturing growth especially of corporate culture
Healed	Turned around
Death	Bankruptcy/ Close down/ Wind up
Undertaker	Liquidator
Heart	Mindset/ Attitude
Heart Attack/ Stroke	Major Business failure/ Strategic error
Culture	Corporate culture/ Immune system
Internal Energy/ "Qi"	Drive/ Passion
DNA	Business Model

"THERE IS A STRONG PARALLEL BETWEEN PHYSICAL AND FISCAL HEALTH"

Why do Companies Fail

Main signs of impending Business Failures

As per 1998 Survey by Business Planning & Research International for PwC:

- Loss of Market   (29%)
- Management failure (24%)
- Finance   (18%)
- Bad Debts   (10%)
- Competition   (6%)
- Others   (13%)

Troubled companies usually manifest two types of problems – Internal and External – which we discuss as Internal and External Viruses in our Medical Analogy

As per Trend watch Opinion poll by TMA in Dec 2006

Table 1: Industries with Greatest Financial/Operational Difficulty during Year (2007 predicted)

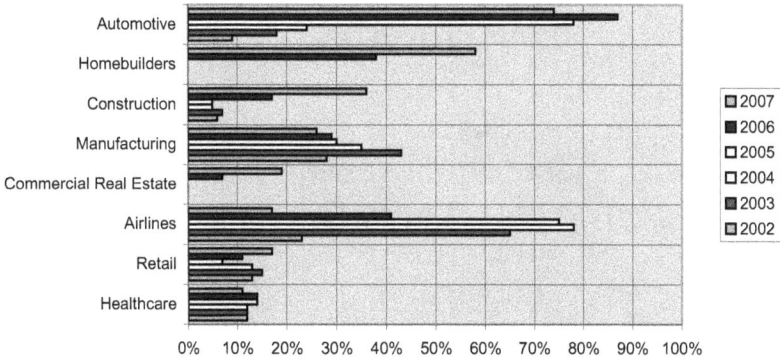

Automotive
Homebuilders
Construction
Manufacturing
Commercial Real Estate
Airlines
Retail
Healthcare

Legend:
- 2007
- 2006
- 2005
- 2004
- 2003
- 2002

0% 10% 20% 30% 40% 50% 60% 70% 80% 90% 100%

Table 2: Reasons for 2007 Underperformance

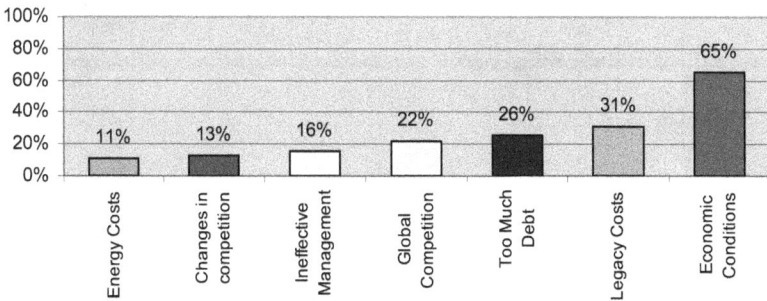

Energy Costs	Changes in competition	Ineffective Management	Global Competition	Too Much Debt	Legacy Costs	Economic Conditions
11%	13%	16%	22%	26%	31%	65%

Source: Turnaround Management Association

In almost all these causes of failures, we can see that the problems could have been avoided with proper futuristic planning.

Therefore, an old Proverb said:

"The superior doctor prevents sickness. The mediocre doctor attends to impending sickness. The inferior doctor treats the actual sickness"

You do not have to get sick to get better.
Anonymous

Internal and External Corporate Viruses

INTERNAL	EXTERNAL
Management Problems	
- Arrogance - Procrastination - Incompetent CEOs/ Managers - Resistance to change - Poor quality staff - Lapses in internal control	Government intervention/ regulations Economic recession Political turmoil
Bad Financial Control	
- Cash flow - Accounting system behaviour - Budgetary control	Appreciating/ depreciating currencies Changes in consumer
Operational Weaknesses	
- High costs - Weak logistics - Bad marketing	Environmental/ health issues Technological changes
Human Resource Problems	
- Negative attitudes - High staff turnover materials - Other factors	Natural disasters Shortage of workers/ raw Labour unrest
Major Project Fiasco	
- Over leveraging	Terrorist attacks

The Era of Competition

➤ 1970s and 1980s – Management Mantra was product quality. Quality Circles (QC), Total Quality Management (TQM), and ISO9000 were the order of the day

➤ 1980s and 1990s – Management Slogan embraced Technology as the cure-all

➤ 2001 collapse of high-tech NASDAQ stocks meant – Technology is only a channel; what matters is Management and People

➤ In the new Millennium focus has shifted to COMPETITION

> **Every new change forces all the companies in an industry to adapt their strategies to that change.**
>
> **Bill Gates**

Corporate Rescue Treatment can be classified into three phases:

➢ **Phase - I: Surgery** - Primary focus on restructuring the organization and improving the cash flow

➢ **Phase - II: Resuscitation-** Efforts concentrating on revitalizing the business' top-line and profit

➢ **Phase - III: Nursing -** Rehabilitating a strong and healthy corporate immune system for sustained long-term growth

COMPLETE CORPORATE TURNAROUND PLAN

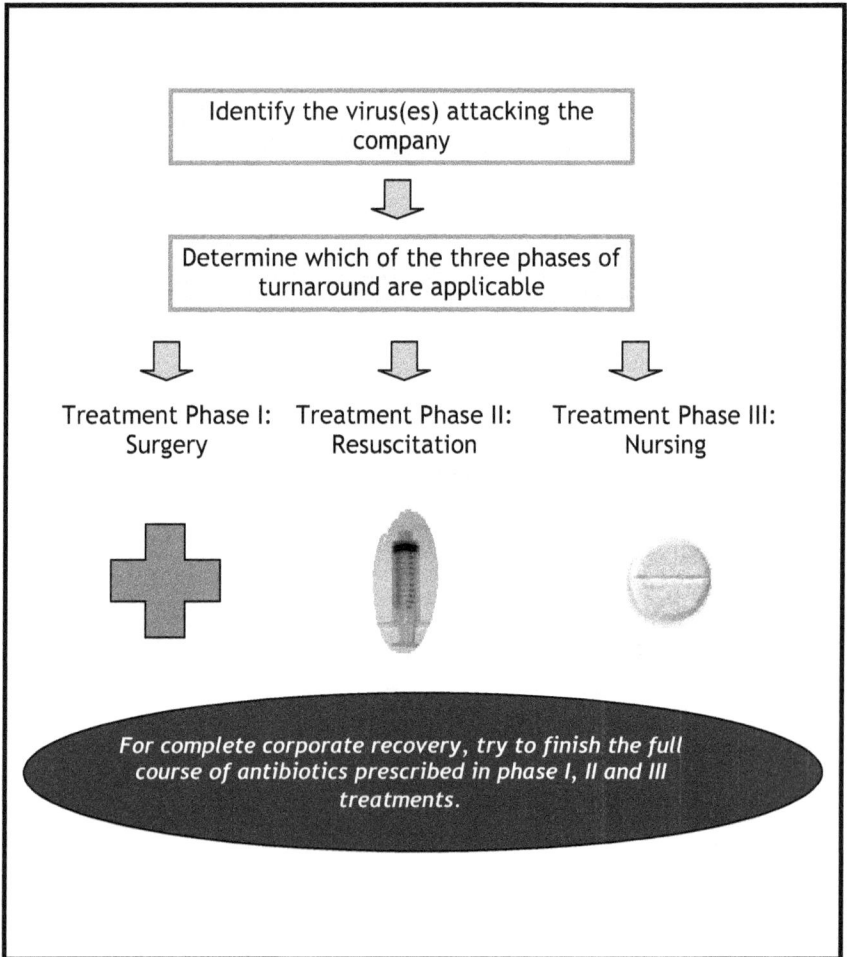

Identify the virus(es) attacking the company

⬇

Determine which of the three phases of turnaround are applicable

⬇   ⬇   ⬇

Treatment Phase I: Surgery   Treatment Phase II: Resuscitation   Treatment Phase III: Nursing

For complete corporate recovery, try to finish the full course of antibiotics prescribed in phase I, II and III treatments.

Illustration

Capsules

On

Corporate Illness

Internal Virus – Causing Corporate Illness – Case of Ansett, Australia

An example of the importance of having a good CEO is illustrated through Ansett, Australia's number two domestic carriers. Ansett Australia is suffering from financial woes and unable to find a financial savior. It is hemorrhaging at A$1 million a week, with its debts estimated at more than A$2 billion (US$1 billion).

Its founder Reginald Ansett grew the airline from modest beginnings in 1936. Sir Reginald, who was knighted for the success of Ansett, was the driving force behind Ansett's rise. In 1979, non-airline industry players, Rupert Murdoch's News Ltd and transport company TNT bought the Ansett airline and pushed Sir Reginald into a figurehead position until his death in 1981. The absence of Sir Reginald left the airline without a strong leader. The new owners were not in the industry for the long term and made several bad decisions about its plane fleet and also implemented detrimental cost-cutting exercises to trim the operations in preparation for a profitable sale. Air New Zealand bought a 50 percent stake from TNT in 1996 but it was too late to save Ansett. The problems were further compounded in 2001 by a series of embarrassing maintenance oversights that led to the grounding of its entire fleet of ageing Boeing 767s, further eroding public confidence in the airline. Ansett was subsequently overwhelmed by the internal viral attack of poor management. The loss of a strong CEO (Sir Reginald) coupled with the incompetence of his successors caused the downfall of Ansett.

Sometimes, a blood transfusion or surgery is required to change the whole management team and eliminate the internal viruses. The medical analogy for eliminating internal viruses may merit the use of Western medical treatments such as vaccination or surgery which calls for a standardised, invasive, scientific and analytical approach. The equivalent of this in the corporate context would be downsizing, restructuring, new market development, etc. The key is that one must administer the medicine quickly before the patient takes a turn for the worse.

External Viruses – Example of IBM in 1990

The external viruses are harder to eliminate because these are generated from outside the organisation. Sometimes even having a strong management team will not help to eradicate the external viruses totally. Thomas J. Watson the head of IBM, in his book *A Business and Its Belief* told an interviewer that he was afraid IBM would become a big and inflexible organisation that would not be able to keep up with the changes in the computer industry. He said these 30 years before the arrival of Bill Gates and Steve Jobs. Watson was right. IBM (pre-Gerstner's days) almost went bust in the 1990s. Although mighty IBM had a highly motivated and skilled management team coupled with a very strong brand reputation, it could not withstand the

onslaught of personal computers. Then IBM had a corporate culture of arrogance and ignored the threats of personal computers to its own peril. For instance, Gates approached IBM several times during the early days of Microsoft for some collaboration. IBM rejected them all and perhaps could have owned Microsoft today if some of Gates' proposals were accepted as he was then vulnerable to an acquisition bid by IBM. When IBM woke up to the serious threat of PC, Gates was financially much stronger and unwilling to part with Windows.

IBM was fortunate in its timely recruitment of Lou Gerstner as chairman and CEO to rescue IBM. Many others were not so lucky. The data bore out the demise of other major companies. For example, of the Fortune 500 companies of 1970, only a third exists today. Many went by the wayside because of their inability to cope with change caused by the attacks of external viruses. The treatment to administer in order to eradicate external viruses is to foster a strong and healthy corporate culture, which is the immune system of the company. The immune system produces antibodies to eradicate the viruses.

Need for Early Diagnosis - The Case of Kin

Self-diagnosis and treatment provides a good business for bankruptcy lawyers and undertakers.

Let's call him Kin: Kin was a CEO of a fine company. He used experts that were experienced, capable, and trusted to help him keep his company healthy. But he was not feeling well. At his last physical, his liver tested in the questionable range.

He was not a drinker, and was careful to take his multi-vitamins daily. Even though he was 60, he played a tough game of tennis. He read all he could on how to make his liver recover: drinking dandelion tea, tomatoes, eating more liver, which was one of his favorite foods, and no more alcohol. He took more vitamins and his

iron and other levels were above average; in fact his iron level was quite remarkable. His wife and the corporate board members urged him to seek an expert at the Mayo Clinic, a famed clinic for difficult cases and diseases.

What he found out through the help of a world-renowned physician was a shock. What he was doing to treat himself was suicide. He was killing himself through his own mouth. His body overproduced iron, and like filings of steel this overproduction attacked his organs and began destroying them over time. To make it worse and a fatal condition, the usual harmless daily multi-vitamin's iron load was a huge mistake. His liver was irreparable—it was too far gone to ever work normally again. He learned the liver was essential to almost everything in his total body. He faced a certain death. The diagnosis was that he had the genetic condition of hemochromatitis. This inherited condition, mainly running in European blood lines is largely undiagnosed or misdiagnosed, and millions die from this silent killer every year. But he now knew what the cause of his death would be.

Through the human kindness of a cyclist who was killed on his motorcycle, and who donated his organs for helping others, Kin received a transplant: a life and death turnaround. Kin is a thankful and smiling CEO again.

What a struggling company often needs is what Kin needed. Without the expert's eyes, ears, and training he would have died undiagnosed or the guesses would all have been wrong. His self-care was commendable, and in no way does Kin's case oppose self-care: He would have died much earlier, or missed becoming an acceptable transplant candidate, if he hadn't taken good care of himself in controllable areas by keeping fit and informed.

We move down a decision tree in making a correct diagnosis of a company's health. Some companies are sick because there are many things wrong with them. In surgery there are times when the patient has reached the end, the diagnosis has been made, the cutting stopped, and hopefully the patient will have some time to reflect on his life with pain monitoring before saying goodbye.

Change management must prioritize its steps carefully and make sure they have made a clear and accurate picture of the patient, the company's ailments, otherwise several years could be wasted and the patient made worse or untreatable. Repeated needs for surgery are bad omens of news. A time will be reached when the only help cannot be given because the patient cannot stand the help one more time.

Focusing the turnaround management and change capital on the best bang for the buck might be the best shot, to instill confidence of change in the company that is struggling. The patient that holds hope will always do better. The diagnostic approach is good for more than once: it needs to be institutionalised for the company to handle changes in the future. It is part of the recovery.

The Case of Minco

The middle-sized company of Minco from the middle of the US is in a highly competitive business of medical and aeronautical technology and found they could not meet their customer needs. Many of their customers were in the Asia/Pacific market area and demands were made for customization of their product they could not provide. Loss of sales and profits were at stake—and worse—the loss of a faithful customer base in Asia/Pacific. In June of 2006, under expert advice, they researched the best country in the Asia/Pacific market area for them to quickly establish a design and service center. Because of Singapore's record for smooth corporate operations, such as the ability to exchange currencies freely, and the nation's considerable medical and aeronautical technology resources, they chose Singapore. Instead of lost sales they are now reporting increased sales (www.minco.com).

Section -3

Phase - I: Surgery

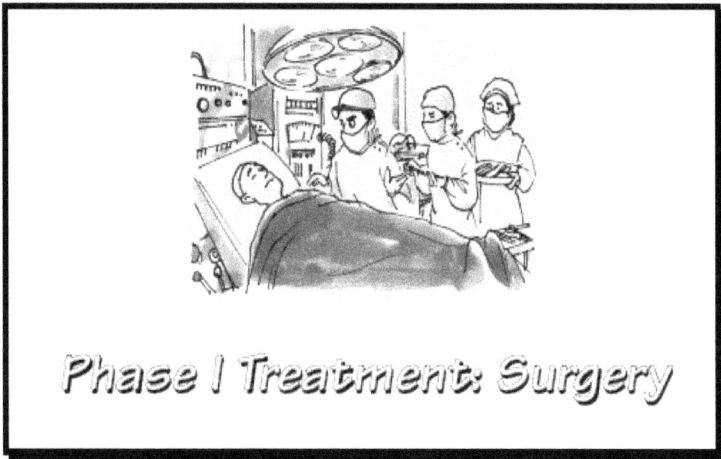

Phase I Treatment: Surgery

Company A - Local Company with Cancer

- Background : Local SME-Trading, Manufacturing of industrial products
- Problems : Losing market share/ margins, High overheads, Unfocused
- Direction : Jack of all trades, Master of none
- Orientation : Unsystematic
- Management Style : Laissez-faire
- Structure : No regard for profitability
- Communication : Each department doing its own thing

3.2 The need for a Surgical Phase

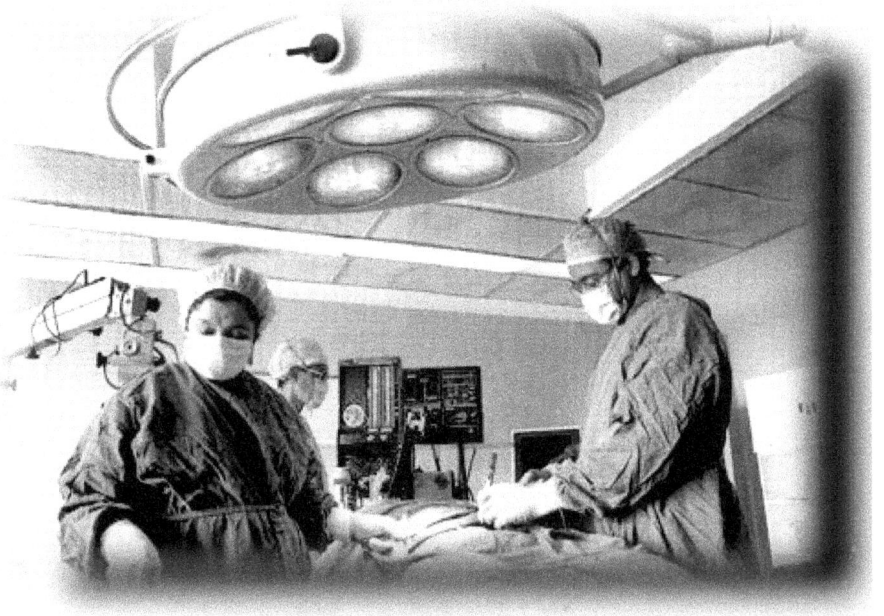

Surgery or corporate restructuring is not
a burn-and-slash
Exercise but calls for the surgeon's
skills.

PHASE -I
SURGERY - RESTRUCTURING THE ORGANISATION

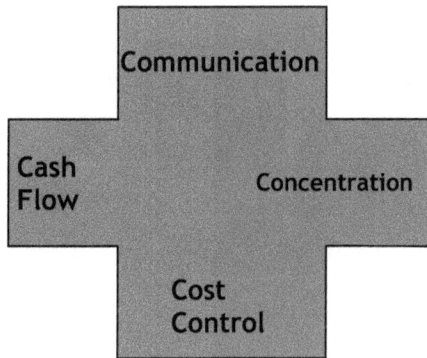

Communication

Cash
Flow

Concentration

Cost
Control

Remember the 4Cs in corporate surgery.

Three Tenets of Communication

- ➢ **Form a Turnaround team:** The first step to creating a successful change is to get everyone on board. If they believe that what you are doing will lead to a better future, the employees will make an effort to ensure that these changes work

- ➢ **Enlist Support:** Autonomy is often not given. You have to earn the trust and support of various parties

- ➢ **Apply a No-nonsense Management Style:** Participative and Consensus Management is not likely to work during Phase – I.

> Andrew Grove who led the turnaround of Intel said:
>
> *"What is 'nice' or 'not nice' should have no place in how you think or what you do. Remember we are after what is most effective"*

Remember the Golden Rule in
Communication during the Surgery Phase:

*"The turnaround CEO
needs to personally
talk to the staff. Just
as a Doctor does not
ask the Nurse to talk
to the patient"*

Concentration

> During the Surgical phase, there is always a severe constraint on *Time* and *Resources*.

> Hence the need to concentrate all the resources on doing a few major things right.

> You need laser-sharp focus just as a Surgeon focuses on just only one operative field during surgery.

> This C entails administration of the four Tools of Concentration

The Four Tools of Concentration:

- *Focusing on Core Competence*

- *Eliminating marginally profitable projects*

- *Adopting a zero-based budgeting approach*

- *Challenging past business assumptions*

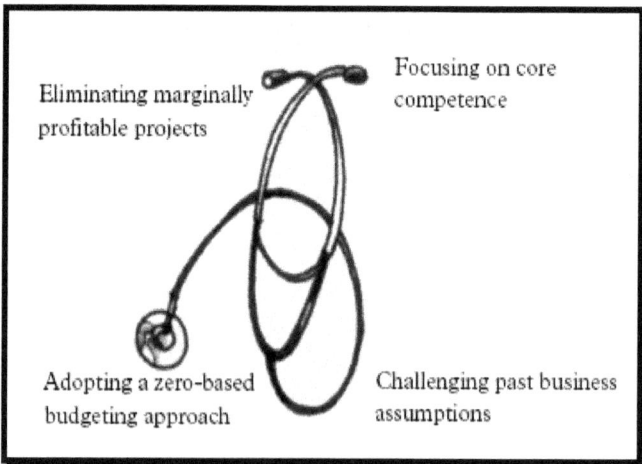

Eliminating marginally profitable projects

Focusing on core competence

Adopting a zero-based budgeting approach

Challenging past business assumptions

3.3.3 - Cost Control

- ➤ Cost Control is an important antidote to administer, especially in desperate turnaround situations

- ➤ For successful implementation of cost control, the cuts must be swift, strong and decisive

- ➤ Since it involves many unpopular decisions, it must be carried out in a sensitive and yet prudent manner

- ➤ The key here is knowing how to cut costs without hurting the already ailing company further

The three main categories of Cost Control:

- Cutting Operating Budgets

- Downsizing Workforce

- Reducing fixed and variable overheads

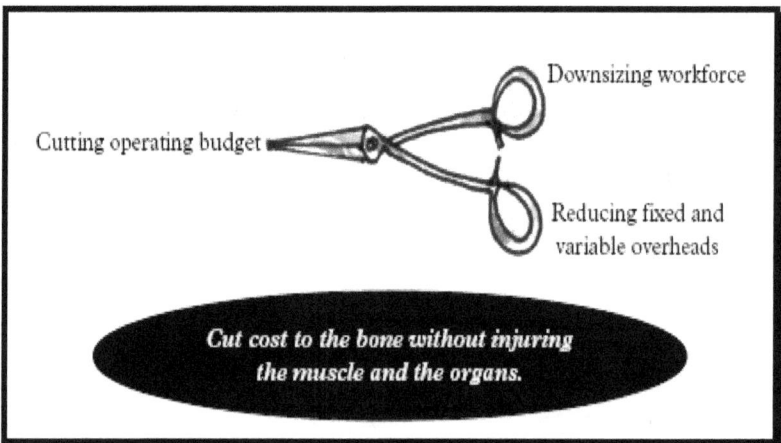

Cutting operating budget — Downsizing workforce — Reducing fixed and variable overheads

Cut cost to the bone without injuring the muscle and the organs.

Downsizing is like amputation which removes part of a body.

Getting rid of dysfunctional personnel is like a cancer operation, make sure that the tumour does not come back again.

Treat the employee to be fired well, for one day it might be you.

Win back the trust after a downsizing exercise.

3.3.4 - Cash Flow

➢ Cash Flow constitutes the Life Blood of a Company

➢ It is a vital resource for the Company's successful management and healthy operations

➢ Slipping into losses may give you a headache, but a sudden shortfall in cash flow will cause immediate massive migraine

➢ The approach should be two-pronged - Boosting cash receipts, and reducing cash outflows / expenses

This last C is an indispensable ingredient in the Turnaround Plan, and entails:

- Selling off unrelated businesses and non-core assets

- Controlling Inventory levels

- Reducing Purchases / Perks

- Reviewing and Renegotiating Terms

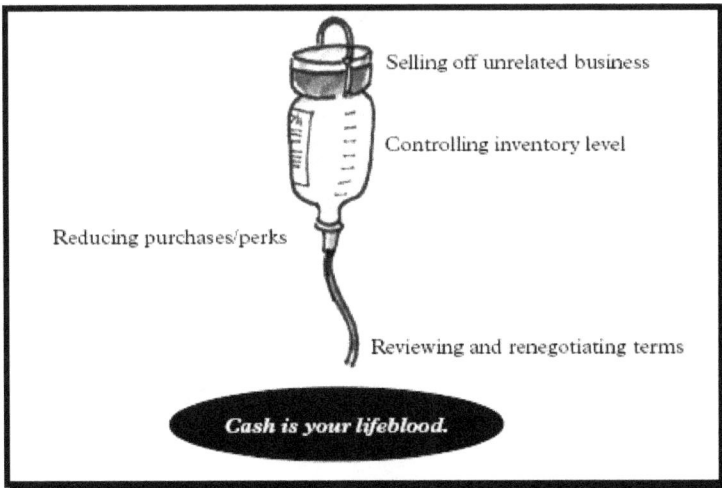

Selling off unrelated business

Controlling inventory level

Reducing purchases/perks

Reviewing and renegotiating terms

Cash is your lifeblood.

Illustration

Capsules

On

Surgery Phase

Need for Communication - British Petroleum

In August of 2006 a major oil spill occurred in the largest oil producing area of North America. At the same time the price of petroleum had reached a record high on the world market and prices for fuel had almost doubled in some areas. Bankruptcies shot up, and airline flights were limited because of high energy costs. It was a bad time to be throwing oil in the ocean. The worldwide press coverage put the company British Petroleum in a bad light. As is usual, the common approach was taken and the CEO was moved, but all agreed that a turnaround had to occur so this would not happen again. A new CEO was quickly hired and the former CEO moved to a second position in the company at Alaska.

This Prudhoe Bay, Alaska, petroleum operation under the direction of the new CEO instigated an immediate investigation of what went wrong. The findings showed that the spill was caused by careless maintenance operations and management, causing damage.

To solve the maintenance and management problem the new CEO decided the causes were internal, and could only be solved by better communication within the company. The new CEO established a blog site for the employees to discuss how the company could improve its operations, and in addition, retained outside and independent turnaround and environmental experts to determine how to solve the problem.

The result was that BP accomplished the clean up, repair, and implementation of a new safety and engineering program in one-half the time it would normally take.

Kia Motors – Leadership and mgt style in turnaround

Kia Motors, Korea made a stunning turnaround and accelerated from a deficit of 7 trillion won (US$6.2 billion) to a surplus of 180 billion won in a single year (2000). It moved from court receivership in less than 24 months. The Kia vice president Uhm Sung-yong told Suh Hae-sung of the *Asia Times* that the answer was "tough restructuring". Apparently the number of employees was cut 30 percent to 29,000 from 40,000 and five companies were merged into one. New funds were also provided by Hyundai who took it over in 1998 when it was flat.

The Hyundai Group chairman personally oversaw Kia's operations, touring production lines as often as possible and encouraging employees. This merger was a clear success and an asset to both companies, yet each retained their own individuality. Strong leadership in a time of difficulty made the difference.

Hong Kong – based Family Business Case – Need for professionalism

A Hong Kong listed company, managed by the major shareholder, the chairman, and his family was initially a garment manufacturer, they expanded into other related businesses and one not so related—property management ventures in the PRC. Although the garment business grew over the years as their core business, the management evolved to members of the family who were inexperienced, particularly in accounting and finance management.

The chairman and another member of the company had good contacts in the new project area, but the development team was without property development experience. The company took on a major office and residential project, however, as they were beginning the development the property values in the site areas fell, which lessened the security values on the property held by their bankers. In addition, the company faced stiff competition in its core business, the garment industry, and cash flow forced the company to go to its financial limits, worrying the bankers more. An assessment of the company's health situation was made, and these are the findings: Poor management by family members destroyed the formal reporting structure and this needed to be rehabilitated. This caused many competent managers to leave. Management was resistant to change. The company's information processes and accounting systems were sub-standard. There were no management accounts or forecasts. Finally, there was a total lack of management of stock, inventory and obsolescence ratings.

For a successful turnaround the following changes were required: Restoration of the information systems and monitoring to achieve proper management control; competent and professional management; a clear marketing strategy focusing on the competitive advantage of the company's core businesses; reduction of operating costs to a level that will work for the longer term. A capital structure needed to be implemented that would meet the future requirements of the business. The operating and other efficiencies tended to go along with production planning, machine production and updated technology. Important as well was the need to rid themselves of non-core

businesses by selling them off and improving their cash flow. And as we have stated earlier in this book there must be a correct mix of professional advice and that often extends beyond accountants and lawyers. There will have to be compromises as the turnaround team moves the recovery along.

Focusing on Core Competence - Examples of IBM, GE, Microsoft, and Creative

In an increasingly competitive business environment, the sick company must return to the basics. It needs to concentrate and focus on its core competence, instead of being distracted by the urge to venture into new areas in order to survive. This is usually the only option left for the sick company as it lacks the financial resources to venture into non-core areas.

Michael Porter identified one of the competitive strategies as focusing the firm's limited resources on one or a few product-market segments.

IBM

Furthermore one lesson learnt by IBM's turnaround CEO, Lou Gerstner, was: "Don't assume you must move into new business areas to succeed. You often can succeed – at far lower cost – by doing a better job with the businesses and skills you already have." Before the arrival of Gerstner in 1993 as chairman and chief executive, Wall Street had speculated that IBM was heading for bankruptcy or breakup. Most new business have start-up costs, resulting in operating losses which an ailing company can ill-afford. Also, valuable resources may need to be deployed to handle such new ventures, thereby further weakening the company's strength. This is the time for serious evaluation and prioritising – putting first things first.

GE

In order to free up resources for its core business, the ailing company has to divest any unprofitable or non-related businesses. This view is also affirmed by Jack Welch, the ex-chairman of General Electric (GE) (US) who demanded that GE's businesses had to be first or second in their market, or they would be radically reformed, sold or closed. Scores were shut. GE's workforce came down by 100,000. Yet, Welch created more shareholder value on the face of the planet than any other CEO.

Microsoft

Microsoft has every one of its employees 100-percent focused on dominating each market it targets. Just as no one has ever given his or her life for two causes, Microsoft believes that no employee can give fair and equal attention to two different projects. With rare exceptions, each employee at Microsoft has one major task. For a vice president, that task may be to take over the entire desktop application market.

Creative

Sim Wong Hoo, Chairman and CEO of Creative Technology, Singapore (the largest PC audio manufacturer in the world) was refocusing and reorganising his business, chastened by a substantial loss of US$130.4 million for its fiscal year ended June 2001. Primarily to blame was a foray into high-tech investments that initially brought huge returns but with the collapse of tech stocks worldwide, resulted in net investment losses and write-downs of almost US$150 million for the year. Hence the refocus on PC audio and the Sound Blaster family of sound cards in particular. Sim explained: "Recently, we did some very deep soul-searching, crunching all the numbers again. We found that if we had just focused on audio alone, we would have been a much more profitable business. Every time we tried to stretch and move out of the audio space, these new businesses were only so-so. We could have done without them." He argued: "I think there is a lesson to learn in that when times are bad we need focus. There's actually big money to be made even in a downturn if we are very focused in an area where we are very strong."

Challenging past Business Assumptions

Time and time again, some wrong business assumptions and perceptions by experts have led many companies astray.

Mercedes-Benz missed out on opportunities in small cars because in their research prediction of Mercedes-Benz in 1900, it was found that "worldwide demand for a car will never exceed one million primarily because of a limitation in the number of available chauffeurs."

Ken Olson, president of Digital Equipment said in 1977: "There is no reason anyone would want a computer in their home." Even Thomas Watson, chairman of IBM said in 1943: "I think there is a world market for about five computers."

Another chairman of IBM, John Akers added in 1983: "The world market for computers is about 275,000."

Owing to these erroneous perceptions, no wonder both Digital Equipment and IBM were late in entering the personal computer market.

Even so-called experts had been proven wrong. Margaret Thatcher said during a TV interview in 1977: "No, I cannot see a woman prime minister in my lifetime." Two years later, she became the first lady prime minister of the United Kingdom and was voted in as prime minister for three terms (1979–90).

The US Pentagon with thousands of high level staff on intelligence work made this remark two days before Iraq invaded Kuwait: "Saddam is bluffing, there is no way he will attack."

To ensure its effective and successful implementation, the turnaround CEO must critically re-examine and revisit every business assumption made by the company in the past. Functioning much like diagnostic tests such as blood tests, this will initiate a sifting process to identify which of these assumptions actually contributed to the distressed company's existing woes and conundrum.

Divesting to Improve Cash Flow

One effective way to improve cash flow is to liquidate and sell off the company's non-core businesses and assets.

Siam Cement, a blue chip Thai conglomerate borrowed heavily in US dollars for its expansion. When the baht collapsed in 1997, its foreign debt escalated to US$5 billion. Consequently, Siam Cement had to offload more than 40 subsidiaries to keep the company afloat, selling off non-core businesses such as steel foundries, car parts factories and glass production plants. In the year 2000, Siam Cement recorded its first positive financial results since 1997 after divesting its non-core businesses. Today, Siam Cement is hailed as a model for troubled Thai companies.

Another successful corporate turnaround after divesting its non-core assets and businesses is Neptune Orient Line (NOL). In 1997, NOL acquired APL, a leading shipping line and shortly later the Asian financial crisis struck, resulting in NOL's financial losses in 1997 and 1998. To address its financial woes NOL took the bold steps of selling off its headquarter building, US train network and properties in several countries. NOL also closed its loss-making joint ventures in China. In 1999, NOL rebounded strongly when the Asian economy recovered.

Renegotiating with Customers and Suppliers for better cash flow and profitability – The strategy of a mid-size company

Cutting off credit to a business is like ending blood flow to an organism. Once a bank acts in this way, the expectation is the company will go under. What can be done? A middle sized family owned Tool Company had an answer, but it took nearly three years to recover. The bank's final advice was a suggestion to the CEO to retain an accountant who specialized in turnarounds. He sold some of the company land to pay for the help, which turned out to be a good investment. Other than that he started taking anti-depressant medication, which his doctor ordered.

After a walk through the shop and a review of the books it showed the company was facing a complete meltdown. But the staff was skilled, the CEO was willing to make whatever changes were needed, the customers were always treated well and were loyal to the company, and the plant had good equipment. The expert believed there was hope. This was all laid out in a new proposal to the bank that relented foreclosure a bit. "If our bank forecloses now or in 30 days it won't make much of a difference," the loan officer concluded.

Getting to work quickly, the CEO, staff and the turnaround expert, followed up on the findings:

A cost analysis had showed that while the machines were running, many orders were not particularly profitable. "Our company must not chase revenues and forget about profits," was written on the sales desk bulletin board and it became the gist of a number of meetings with employees. As a result, the team agreed to raise some prices and drop one large customer that was not profitable enough.

To raise cash, they contacted their remaining good customers and the largest supplier. The goal was to get these customers to pay more quickly while the supplier was asked to increase the credit level. On the supply end, the steel company agreed to let the company have $2 worth of product for each $1 paid, up too a given limit, and not charge interest on any bill less than 70 days old. Nearly three years later they were back in the black and on good terms with the bank. And the CEO no longer requires the medication.

A middle-sized business faced another quarter of losing money. "The company wasn't there, and the plan just wasn't there. And there was no energy driving the company," the CEO admitted.

He took action and talked to the creditors: "*We* have a choice. We can blow this thing up today, or we can put in a new plan in place that gives this company a chance. I'm not going to pay you for 90 days. And that's your best shot at getting your money back." And they agreed.

Under their new plan they reduced overhead and management salaries and brought some new designs into production that had been on the back burner, and narrowed their focus on their core business.

The debts have been reduced, the loans current, and the course of losses reversed

Cash flow and Cost Control measures of a Mid-sized company

Section -4

Phase - II

Resuscitation

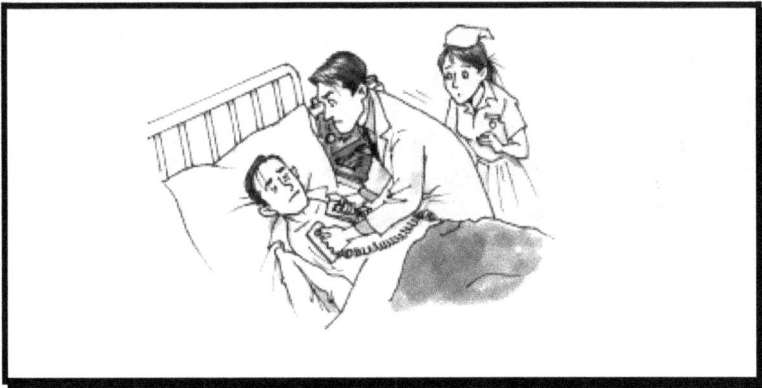

4.1 Multinational Company with a Heart Problem

- Background : Foreign multinational, company contracting & engineering
- Problems : Eroding margins. Loss making. High staff turnover
- Direction : Drifting
- Orientation : Technical, Reactive
- Management Style : Remote, Top-down
- Structure : Conflicts & Infighting
- Communication: Closed, Strong rumour mills

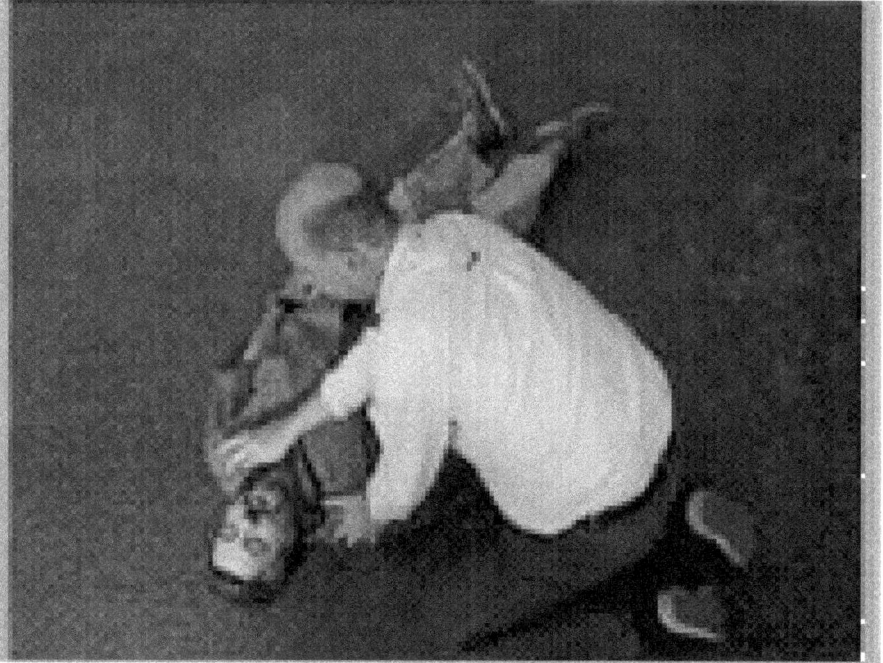

Cardiopulmonary resuscitation can range from price increase to selling an organisation away.

4.2 The Importance of the Resuscitation Phase

➢ The main purpose of the Resuscitation phase is to grow the Business

➢ Cost-cutting exercise is short-term and has limitations

➢ Growing the business is critical to sustain recovery

➢ Companies are like living organisms that need to grow; otherwise they will wither and die

➢ Resuscitation techniques are more marketing-oriented

> **The question about IBM is no longer one of survival. IBM is back, and we're here to stay. The question now is, can IBM grow?**
> **Louis Gerstner**

4.3 The 8 Pillars for Re-vitalising a Business

1) Ascertaining corporate objectives

2) Staying on the ground/using consultants

3) Focusing on the customers and competitors

4) Developing the right product and price

5) Implementing an aggressive marketing strategy

6) Differentiating using service quality

7) Strengthening the Brand Name

8) Investing in future expansions

Objective:		• Ascertaining corporate objectives
Gathering Information:		• Staying on the ground/using consultants (if necessary) • Focusing on customers and competitors
Short-term Strategies:		• Developing the right product and price • Implementing an aggressive marketing strategy
Long-term Strategies:		• Differentiating using services quality • Strengthening the brand name • Investing in future expansions

A good resuscitation strategy is like a good shot of booster.
It can revive a dying business, minus the pains of surgery.

4.3.1 Ascertaining Corporate Objectives

Formulation and Crystallization of corporate objectives is critical for the Resuscitation steps

They steer the company towards the direction it should be heading

In case f the MNC, the Company was making losses despite being No 1 in Sales

In the restructuring process, the corporate objective was clearly stated as - to be No 1 in profitability, not necessarily in Sales

> *"Definiteness of purpose is the starting point of all achievements."*
>
> *Clement Stone*

4.3.2 Staying on the Ground (Using Consultants - if necessary)

Staying on the ground involves the turnaround CEO gathering information first-hand to make wise decisions

External consultants, like therapists, can help companies formulating strategies to venture into new markets and products, Mergers & Acquisitions, promotion of Brand names etc...

There is an old saying in Spain:
To be a bullfighter, you must
first learn to be a bull.
Anonymous

4.3.3 Focusing on Customers and Competitors

➤ The focus of your marketing strategy should be on *Customers and Competitors*

➤ Understand the Strengths and Weaknesses of your Company as well as of the Competitors

➤ Analyse the quadrant you are in, in the Customer-Competition Orientation Matrix

  o Competition-driven
  o Market-driven
  o Customer-driven
  o Internally-driven

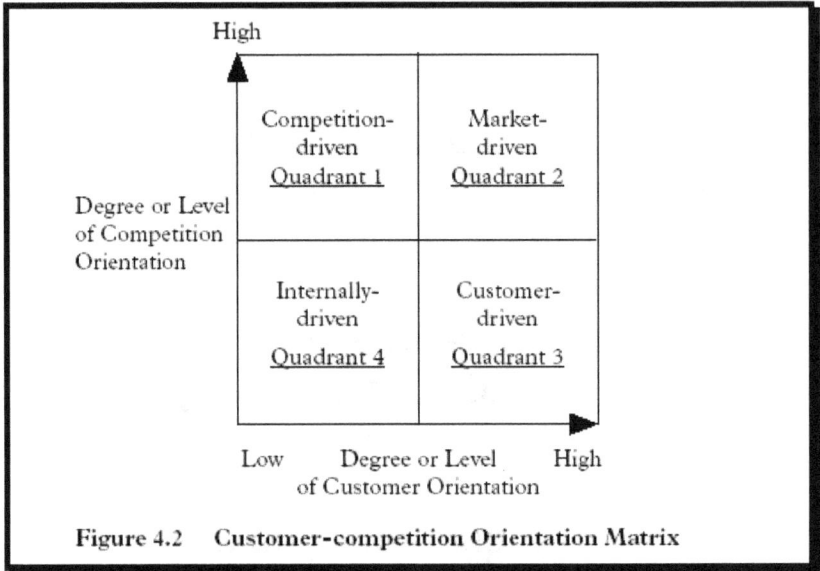

	High	
	Competition-driven Quadrant 1	Market-driven Quadrant 2
Degree or Level of Competition Orientation		
	Internally-driven Quadrant 4	Customer-driven Quadrant 3

Low   Degree or Level   High
of Customer Orientation

Figure 4.2   Customer-competition Orientation Matrix

Companies in Quadrant 1 tend to concentrate too much on staving off competition, resulting in losing sight of Customer needs. - "Win the battle but lose the war"

At the opposite extreme, Companies in Quadrant 3 are extremely customer-driven, to the exclusion of other factors in marketplace dynamics

Companies in Quadrant 4 - Internally-driven orientation are even more pathetic. They are worn out by internal problems - poor workflows, mismanagement, politicking, etc...- And meeting customer needs takes a back-seat.

Marketing Orientation - in Quadrant 2 - is the recommended approach for Companies to adopt. This ensures vibrant business and continued long-term growth

To treat the symptoms, know the competitors and customers.
To eliminate the cause, know the market.

Better understand the market or it will destroy you.

4.3.4 Developing the Right Product and Price

> Having ascertained corporate objectives, and decided on the customer-competitor focus while staying on the ground, the next step for the turnaround CEO is to optimize the product and price mix

> Products that deliver real benefits and performance improvements are the ones that will perk up the customers

> Customers have a broader perception of performance apart from utilitarian benefits

> For some products/services experiential or emotional impact is a prime measure of performance

- Getting a good price for the product is similar to a good mouth-to-mouth resuscitation - easy to administer, and can yield immediate results for the bottom-line

- Right pricing for the target market is important - different geographical segments may need different prices

> While great devices are invented in the laboratory, great products are invented in the marketing department.
> William H. Davidow

> You can have wealth and wisdom but you better have health. Similarly, you can have performance and quality but you better have pricing.

4.3.5 Implementing an Aggressive Marketing Strategy

An aggressive marketing strategy does to a company what a cardiopulmonary resuscitation does to failing human life

The prime objective of the marketing strategy, at this stage is to generate more profitable business.

In the midst of dire difficulties, we may see tendencies of staff wallowing in self-pity, licking their own wounds or playing the game of shame and blame.

E-commerce and Internet marketing are excellent avenues to explore as part of an aggressive marketing strategy during resuscitation

In recession, we need more business, not less.

Some of the key points to remember while implementing a marketing strategy during resuscitation are:

➢Do not downsize your marketing dept too much. In fact, it may be a good idea to poach effective sales executives from your competitors

➢Dispel tendencies among staff to play the blame game, and engage them in some productive activity

➢Explore avenues for e-commerce and internet marketing

➢The key steps related to Internet Marketing, particularly relevant for SMEs, and the corresponding handles (or tools) available on the Internet are as follows:

- Identifying potential Market niche
  - www.wordtracker.com helps in evaluating the effectiveness of keywords
  - www.inventory.overture.com
  - www.goodkeywords.com
  - www.pixelfast.com/overture
  - www.google.com
  - www.ebay.com
  - www.Bigboards.com (for forums)
  - www.Del.icio.us (for bookmarks)
  - www.icerocket.com

- Testing the market niche
  - www.google.adwords.com
  - www.payperclickanalyst.com help ascertaining whether the identified market niche is viable

- o Identifying the right product/service

- o Writing effective Sales Letter
  - Techniques such as
    - Headlines (for Attention)
    - Benefits (to stimulate Interest)
    - USP (to satisfy Desire)
    - Order/Call us (for Action)
  Vendors can be identified at:
    - www.elance.com
    - www.getafreelancer.com
    - www.scriptlance.com
    - www.guru.com
    - www.odesk.com

- o Building a web-site: Effective web design techniques available-
  - Audio/video features
  - Interactive models
  - Customer testimonials

- Squeeze page to capture prospect email addresses
- Domain Name and web-hosting services
  - www.GoDaddy.com
  - www.hostgater.com

- Driving traffic to your website
  - Pay per click advtg through www.google.adwords.com
  - Search Engine Optimisation through
    - Metatags
    - Links
    - RSS feeds
  - Article submission through
    - www.ezinearticles.com
    - www.goarticles.com
  - Blogging through
    - www.wordpress.com
    - www.bloggerspot.com
  - Press Releases through
    - www.prweb.com

- www.prwebdirect.com
  - Ezine Advertisement through
    - www.ezines-R-US.com
    - www.directoryofezines.com
  - Direct Marketing through
    - Customer Databases
    - Auto-responders

- **Monitoring and Fine tuning**

> In times of great stress and adversity,
> it is always best to keep busy, to plough your
> anger and your energy into something positive.
> **Lee Iacocca**

> We are all faced with a series of
> great opportunities brilliantly disguised
> as impossible situations.
> **Chuck Swindoll**

4.3.6 Differentiating using Service Quality

- How the Company handles its customers is often more important than the product per se

- In recent times, churns – customers switching loyalty from you to your competitors – are largely attributable to service quality differentiation

- Developing superior Service Quality culture is a key to building a organization with an healthy immune system

Here are some golden words that reflect the need for differentiation using Service Quality

There are no such things as service industries. There are only industries whose service components are greater or less than those of other industries. Everybody is in service.

Theodore Levitt

Our goal as a company is to have customer service that is not just the best but legendary.

Sam Walton

I think we are waking up every day saying: How can we build a better service for our members?

Steve Case

4.3.7 Strengthening the Brand Name

- In the long run an ailing organization needs to build a strong Brand Name to resuscitate its business

- Marketing is the battling of the mindset to get your brand into your customer's mind – One must realize that customers can only remember a limited number of brands in their minds

- A powerful brand commands high brand equity – one of the most valuable marketing assets

Here are some golden words that highlight the importance of Brand Name for any successful organization:

> Any damn fool can put on a deal, but it takes genius, faith and perseverance to create a brand.
>
> **David Ogilvy**

> Brands will still be brands in the future ... but there will be two successful kinds – big powerful brands and specialist, niche brands.
>
> **Al Ries & Jack Trout**

> Brands will be important and if your brand is not number one or two, you may be kicked out of the market.
>
> **Philip Kotler**

4.3.8 Investing in Future Expansions

- This step generally comes in after the basic resuscitation measures are in place

- Availability of resources is the key to Future Expansions, and this needs to be planned meticulously

- Future Expansions can take the forms of:

    - Expansion in production facilities
    - New Business ventures
    - Mergers & Acquisitions

- Some of the pitfalls to avoid in Merger & Acquisitions are:

  - ✓ No homework done
  - ✓ Wrong timing
  - ✓ Ego Trap
  - ✓ Preference for buying success rather than earnings
  - ✓ Rapid expansion can be fatal

Corporate egotism is the anaesthetic that dulls the business sense.

Illustration

Capsules

On

Resuscitation
Phase

Staying on the Ground – Illustrations from Coca Cola, POSB, IBM

Sometimes recommendations made from third-party perspective could be distorted and rather different from the "ground-level" viewpoint. Classic examples are Coca-Cola and POSB.

Coca Cola

Before Coca-Cola introduced the New Coke, they hired a top agency to help them listen to cola drinkers. In countless taste tests, blindfolded consumers swore up and down that they preferred New Coke over the older version. Based on this information, Coca-Cola introduced New Coke with a huge advertisement budget and lots of fanfare. However, something was amiss during the launch of the New Coke.

Some customers did not like the new concoction and they literally emptied the stores with purchases of the old coke. This "story" was picked up by the media and the issue became one where Coca-Cola was seen to be forcing its customers to go for the New Coke when they actually wanted the traditional old one. Finally, the protests became so intense that stocks of the old coke were depleted and Coca-Cola had to bring back the old coke and renamed it Coca-Cola Classic.

POSB

Another example involved Singapore's DBS Bank.2 Following its merger with POSB (Singapore's national savings bank) in March 1999, and on the advice of its foreign consultants, it was decided that DBS Bank was to be the master brand while POSB was to be dropped, assuming only the status of a subsidiary brand mentioned in signage and the like after the master brand. Therefore, Singapore's favourite bank seemed doom to be relegated to the bin of banking history.

One industry source mentioned that the proposal by the foreign consultants showed that they did not understand the emotional attachment that Singaporeans, many of whom grew up with the bank, had for POSB. "They were coming in cold and did not fully understand the landscape," the source was quoted as saying.

But following a public outcry, DBS Bank admitted that it had been wrong to adopt this recommendation. It decided to not only keep the low-cost banking brand but also to strengthen it.

IBM

Gerstner, the CEO of IBM became IBM's hardest-working salesperson – logging thousands of miles to visit key customers and prospects.

His approach sent an unmistakable message to every employee to be hands-on and gave IBM a new image. By staying in contact with the market, Gerstner was able to make the right decision to turn troubled IBM around.

Understanding Customers and Competitors

With better understanding of the customer and competitors profiles, in the banking industry, allocation of resources for customer service vis-à-vis profitability can produce startling results.

For instance, Adrian J. Slywotzky, *et al.* in *Profit Patterns* noted that for some banks, 30 percent of the customer base generates 130 percent of the profit. Another 30 percent breaks even while the bottom 40 percent generates losses equal to 30 percent of the bank's operating profit. Realising these disproportionate statistics, some banks have taken steps to discourage unprofitable customers and deliberately "redirect" them to the competitors.

Advances in computer technology allow banks to identify and charge such unprofitable customers for services ranging from savings accounts to issuing of cheques. These unprofitable customers generally have two options: either they are charged a fee if their accounts fall below certain balances or they are tacitly "encouraged" to take their banking business elsewhere. And to motivate and retain profitable customers, banks provide tiered programmes that feature incentives for maintaining higher balances such as better interest rates and priority processing of transactions.

Competition-driven Orientation

A preoccupation with "beating" the competitor is myopic because it restricts the company in its operations through a delusion that possibilities are limited (that is, the demise of the competitor is the only solution), thereby denying itself of a full range of exciting uncharted ones.

Therefore, in order to rid itself of such negative preoccupations, the company needs to cast its sights forward instead of merely sideways.

This is affirmed through the review of business history which revealed that many successful companies such as Charles Schwab's discount brokerage services, Dell Computer's price-friendly/mail-order/after

sales service mix and Microsoft's operating software, Windows, are conceived by not being obsessed with the narrow thinking of "killing" the competition.

Instead, they are able to break into uncharted territories by carving out new market niches and creating previously non-existent market possibilities for their own businesses.

Therefore the best competitive orientation is to have no competition.

This can be achieved by not playing the game the way your competitors play the game, but rather by formulating and deploying a distinctive strategy that changes the rules in your favour.

Customer-driven Orientation

Singer Corporation did not realise that its customers valued a simple sewing machine. Its engineers kept adding complex features because they thought these could add value for the home seamstress. However, the sales force was not in touch with the real customers. They were merely listening to the suggestions of selected retailers. By adding more gadgets, Singer was actually innovating for the wrong people.

Therefore, it is important to match what the customer's value with what the company assumes its customers value.

Market Orientation

Companies must not only possess a hands-on feel of the competition and be thoroughly conversant with customer's needs but they must look beyond for greater improvements. For example, healthcare company Baxter often locates its people in offices situated right in hospital-customer sites.

In the emerging knowledge-based economy, mass production, mass marketing, mass distribution, etc., are insufficient in meeting customers' needs. Merely providing what consumers want is largely based on past experiences of providing for what people want or like today, however, providing for what they want in the future is often more critical. In order to stay ahead of competition, a successful company must prepare for tomorrow's opportunities by exploiting the "latent needs" of customers. The "latent needs" can be defined as what the customers might truly value but have never experienced or verbalised these desires. What does this mean to companies? They should not be merely led by customers' needs but lead them to demand for the company's products and services by driving the market.

One company that consistently practises this is Microsoft. Besides studying what customers say about their problems with its products and stay tuned in to what they want, they extrapolate future requirements from information garnered from leading-edge buyers. Bill Gates said: "Our customers are always upping the ante, as they should." In the book, *Business @ The Speed of Thought*, Gates was quoted as saying: "You can't just look at the past or current state of the market. You also have to look at where it's likely to go and where it might go under certain circumstances, and then navigate your company based on your best predictions."

The difficulty about following the customer is that the customer often has to be led. Indeed, the great breakthrough for Microsoft came, not from responding to customer demands, but from anticipating them. Microsoft is successful because it is market-driven. Before Windows appeared, only Apple Mac users would have envisioned it. But Apple waited for the feedback from its customers and let Microsoft steal valuable leads.

There are other countless examples of such successes.

For example 3M's Post-It® notes are now one of the most commonly used office products. The assortment of Post-It® stationery and other products helped 3M to generate a cool US$600 million from a market which nobody had asked for.

The 1980 launch of CNN by Ted Turner is another case in point. When it was introduced, Turner was ridiculed by TV veterans and the three big TV stations – CBS, NBC and ABC. They had failed to tap a niche which no one asked for – a 24-hour news service, alternative information viewing option, cable network, etc.

Peter Drucker noted that the Japanese were able to take the lead on fax machines as they were able to ask themselves: "What is the market for what this machine does?" Therefore, each new day presents the creative managers with numerous fresh ideas and responses to tap upon as the dynamic marketplace is full of clues and signals heralding future winners.

The new breed of customers in the new millennium will be attracted to companies who understand that business is no longer about buying and selling products and services. It is about addressing the customer's intangible and latent motives and desires. The new order for the day is dictated by the total experience which includes existing and latent desires of the customers with the company as well as its representatives. Another important aspect of market-driven orientation apart from understanding the customer's present and future needs, is knowing the strategies to combat competition in the present and future. This is especially critical in this competitive era.

Turnaround through R&D and new product lines – the Kodak Case

In 2003 Kodak was facing financial disaster. Although its Asian operations were growing, the company was bleeding in the U.S. and Europe from considerable loss of sales to competitors. The investors and creditors put great pressure upon the company. Their position was that this once great imaging company could not make it in the digital world because it started too late, and competition, particularly from Japan had taken over its market share in core equipment and services. The demand upon management was to use its free cash for dividends and propping up a dying business as long as possible before liquidation or sell-off. The change management team and the CEO developed

a different plan and against heave odds stuck to it: They would sell the former cash cow part of the business, such as cameras etc., except in the Asia and Latin American markets--cut the proposed dividends by seventy some per cent, and plow US$3 billion into research and development in the digital market. Courage and a clear plan of action saved the company, and it developed into a competitor again in the digital world marketplace with considerable performance improvements in growth and profits. The bets are that it sails back from the doldrums.

Importance of Product Design in Turnaround – The Toyota Case

One of the world's most successful companies at design and product development alliances and cooperation with other companies is Toyota from Japan. In the beginning phase, a company may start with a project working on low value products offshore. The goals are usually to reach a lower cost of production, innovation for the product, and also enhance its life cycle. The goal is to stay away from expensive added payroll and bricks and mortar investments in a lean time for the company. A Toyota representative at the Toyota plant in Valenciennes, France, told a reporter from the New York Times in the summer of 2006 that the Toyota French factory, besides bringing on board new designs, would help convince Europeans it is an acceptable product to own and would give Toyota a greater presence in Europe where its sales are starting to grow.

Although the design and production site in Europe is a risk for Toyota, their sales in Europe are climbing as they are in the US, and Toyota according to their manager has for many years had the practice of global design and product development with different factories and companies around the world.

And in many countries, including the United States and the European countries, the consumers are demanding the latest in environmental technology. Engineers from such countries of India and China recognize this in their innovations. The demand for the latest in environmental technology means that current products must be redesigned—the global product development team process can be the answer. A newly designed and environmentally advanced data storage product from India that could replace the current storage disks is one example. And all of this is done at lower costs than if it were attempted at the western company's home site. This alone is a crucial factor in turnaround action.

Right Product at Right Price - Taiwan's BenQ strategy – Do not hurt your own customer

Taiwan companies have been the leading producers of supporting components to the world's well known companies with globally recognized brands, particularly in the manufacturing areas of LCD monitors, PC notebooks, and PDAs. The profits, however, on these products that are branded in the customer name have been drastically falling. Companies in this picture in Taiwan are faced with threatening losses. Competitively, they cannot demand more for their product from their customers. If they attempted to establish their own brands, which would be a turnaround program, they would have to be very careful not to antagonize their core customers by competing against them. It is very difficult to solve this problem and it can very soon lead to major business failures if not turned around for a company.

One Taiwan company that is trying to turn this squeeze position around has this solution that it hopes will work: They purchased a globally recognized brand named product (Siemens) with the right to use the major brand name for a period of years (5) while they (BenQ's), and the product they purchased rights to is not in direct competition with their core customers' products of which they provide. Other Taiwan companies are beginning to

follow a similar program out of the profit squeeze while they still can, for example TVP, which purchased part of the Netherlands's Philips Company's computer display business, making TVP the largest computer display manufacturer in the global market. These preventive measures it is hoped will bring success and endorse principle of not waiting until the temperature rises and the blood pressure falls.

Staying on the Ground (with help from a Consultant) – Case of a Cellular Carrier Company

A large cellular carrier found itself in a fast-deteriorating situation with respect to new signups, churn and bottom line performance following a period of fast growth driven by aggressive acquisitions of other cellular properties. The question was why were things going wrong at a time when cellular industry penetration was on the upswing? And, once the causes were identified, what should be done to turn things around?

Company management felt the firm should be well positioned for growth. They had gambled a significant amount of investment capital by buying up many smaller properties whose performance was expected to improve as a result of the acquiring company's efficiencies of scale and marketing clout. The strategy seemed sound, given the company's aggressive pricing strategy and strong retail presence in new and legacy local markets.

The pricing and marketing plan seemed sure to generate strong profits with reasonable volume growth and low churn. However, failure to achieve anticipated penetration targets produced an ARPU (average revenue per user) that was well below the industry average; this, in turn, led to significant misses on ROI projections from one quarter to the next. This resulted in a plunge in company share prices and an outcry from investors demanding that something be done.

With a worsening crisis and no clear definitions of the company's problems or solutions, management sought professional third-party assistance from Consultant XYZ. While this company's situation represented an extreme case of underperformance compared to that of most cellular companies, Consultant XYZ's efforts offer a comprehensive picture of the many processes and innovative problem solving approaches that Consultant XYZ can bring to any customer's situation, no matter the scope.

A case in point is the operations review methodology that Consultant XYZ employed for this customer. Virtually any cellular provider can benefit from Consultant XYZ's ability to benchmark a company's pricing, sales, customer service and other key areas of performance against those of its competitors. Companies want to know how they stack up against competitors, but they don't have the depth of knowledge about other players and their performance that's required to make fact-based assessments.

With a deep database and extensive research know-how built over many years of service to the cellular industry,

Consultant XYZ has the resources and perspective that a cellular company requires to keep consistent track of the dynamic shifts in competition and market trends. For example, Consultant XYZ can measure a company's costs per sale against those of others, or tell a company how its sales retention efforts compare on a cost-per-call basis. And, as can be seen in this case, Consultant XYZ's professionals possess the management experience required to forge successful strategies to address virtually any set of challenges.

The CONSULTANT XYZ Solution

To identify the full scope of the issues undermining the customer's success, Consultant XYZ engaged two teams: one from its strategy division, CSMG, and one from its operations consulting group. CSMG provided the expertise for thorough research into existing market conditions at the local and national market levels, using a well-honed set of metrics and processes to benchmark the company's performance against a multitude of parameters. The operations group provided the insight into organizational structure and processes that were essential to identifying and solving core problems.

Together these professional teams provided a comprehensive picture of the client's performance against industry benchmarks and the flaws in its organization and operations execution that impeded its ability to meet financial targets. Along with presenting their results to company management, they used their findings to develop a set of recommendations for an action plan to turn the company around. All of this was accomplished in just eight weeks, providing the company a roadmap to recovery that was as cost effective as it was successful.

Specifically, the findings and recommendations touched on the following areas:

Market Performance

An in-depth study of demographics, competing services and other factors in five regions served by the company found that the company was positioned in markets with strong growth potential; indeed, its recent penetration gains were ahead of national averages. But it was losing market share to competitors. Its ARPU was below par, and churn was excessive. A disproportionate number of its new subscribers were "credit challenged." There were also wide variations in company performance metrics from one market to the next.

While the company was found to be weaker than competitors in some areas, such as data services, range of handsets offered and number of partnership agreements with third-party suppliers of enhanced content and applications, the company was stronger than its competition in more important areas, such as voice service pricing plans and retail presence.

Research into other areas of comparison offered key insights into some of the company's problems. For example, the company was found to have less revenue per employee than many other comparable wireless service providers. Although the company was getting a higher share of new customers through its retail channel than other companies, its average store productivity was sub-par. This suggested that its advantage in retail presence was really a disadvantage in terms of overall sales efficiency.

This was underscored by the fact that, unlike its competitors, the company's agent channel operated at a higher cost than the retail channel. A disproportionate share of bill payments was occurring at the retail store level, which further added to costs. Perhaps most revealing of all was the fact that the company had five to six layers of management above the points of direct sales interface with customers, versus the industry norm of three to four layers.

This comparative market research made it clear that the company's problems were not intrinsic to the state of its markets or offerings; rather, they stemmed from organizational and operational deficiencies. These findings supported the validity of Consultant XYZ's findings with regard to problems with the company's basic structure and operations processes.

Organization and Operations

The overarching problems in company organization were related to inefficiencies in its decentralized approach to management, which stemmed from reliance on regional management infrastructures inherited from purchased properties. Failure to consolidate management and eliminate duplication across the regions was reflected in its shortcomings and sub-par performance in marketing, product development, sales and customer service.

For example, lack of centralized leadership in marketing strategy resulted in reactive, ad-hoc responses to the marketplace with no clear, consistent focus on understanding customer needs, demand for products or product positioning. There was no product development process in place and no one to lead such a process. Similarly, weak sales leadership and a dispersed organizational structure resulted in inconsistent direction, confusing performance and compensation metrics, as well as a vague understanding of the service value proposition on the part of the sales force.

Consultant XYZ developed a plan of action around its observations with recommendations addressing all organizational and operational deficiencies. The plan called for restructuring of marketing, product development, sales and customer care operations, starting with key senior level appointments and consolidation of dispersed local management levels. It also called for an overhaul of the retail store organization, with store closings and changes in operations. We included a wide range of recommendations on operations processes and specific actions that would immediately improve marketing messaging and sales performance.

The plan established a few priorities to be addressed first, providing management with the confidence that the steps most essential to turning the company around would be taken first. These were followed by ongoing efforts to streamline operations touching on all aspects of marketing and sales.

Benefits to the Client

Because Consultant XYZ's approach was supported by extensive benchmarking against industry norms across a wide range of categories, management was able to readily accept our recommendations. Our skilled assessment of market conditions allowed the company to see that it had an opportunity to win rather than lose market share. This gave management the encouragement it needed to take the often-painful steps to restructure.

A radical restructuring was undertaken with outstanding results. Sales began to improve almost immediately and, over the course of the next two years, the company experienced a net sales gain across all markets. Market share grew and churn diminished. Within less than two years of the action plan's inception, the resulting revenue and bottom-line performance gains generated a three-fold increase in stockholder share value.

Every company needs to know where it stands in the market with regard to a multitude of comparative measures and, often, there's a need for third-party insight as to what steps companies can take to improve in areas of sub-par performance, whether in customer care, product development, sales efficiency, marketing strategy or other key operational categories. The outstanding results experienced by this client clearly demonstrate that Consultant XYZ can address virtually any operational issue that a mobile company might have.

Section - 5

Phase - III

Nursing

Phase III Treatment: Nursing

5.1 The Case of a Company with a Weak Immune System

• Background	:	Marketing of services
• Problems	:	Dysfunctional corporate culture lagging behind industry
• Orientation	:	Fire-fighting, "Cannot be bothered" attitude. Not proactive
• Management Development	:	No succession planning
• Training	:	Lip service
• Rewards	:	Favouritism
• Performance Management	:	Tolerant

This company is characterized by the following traits:

- ✓ Very poor service quality lagging behind the industry

- ✓ Low staff morale

- ✓ Management attitude towards staff – myopic

- ✓ Entire corporate environment was tolerant with rewards based on favouritism

Diagnosis was – the organisation's *immune system is very weak* – suffering from *immuno-deficiency*

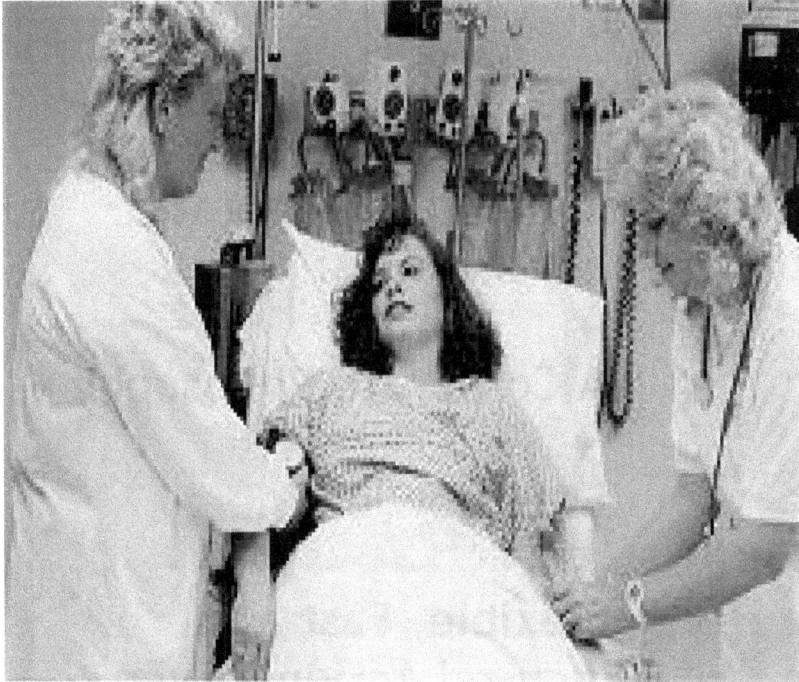

Building a strong and healthy corporate culture is not like having a one-time inoculation.
It is taking vitamin pills for the rest of your life.

5.2 What is the Nursing Phase?

The essence of the Nursing Phase hinges upon the building of a strong and healthy corporate culture that includes:

- ✓ A Corporate Philosophy

- ✓ Free flow of Energy

- ✓ Flexible, Fast and Focused Action-driven orientation

This is best depicted with the following Figure:

Phase III – Nursing: Rehabilitating a Strong and Healthy Corporate Immune System

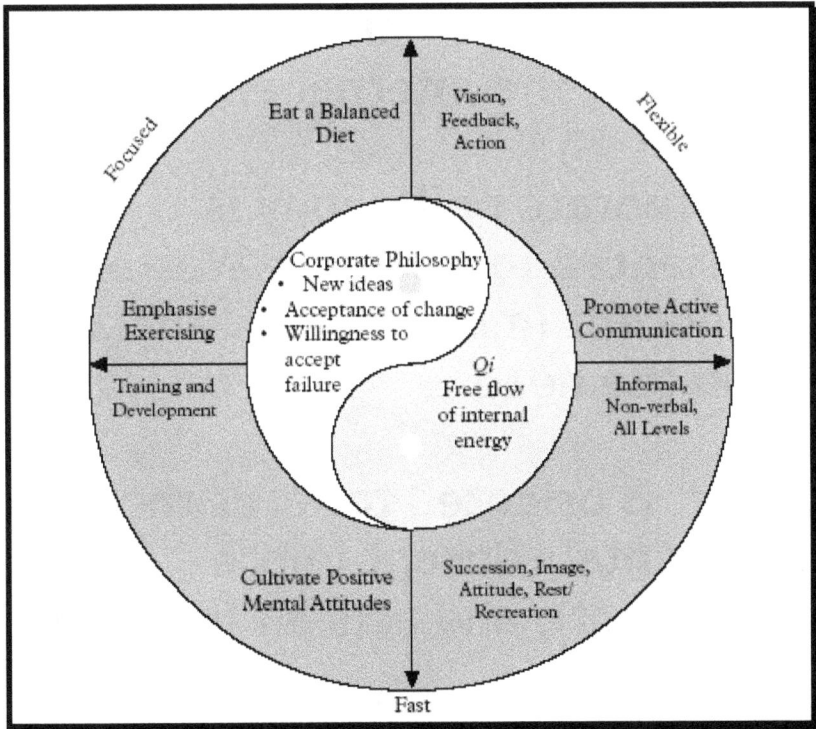

Focused

Flexible

Eat a Balanced Diet

Vision, Feedback, Action

Emphasise Exercising

Training and Development

Corporate Philosophy
- New ideas
- Acceptance of change
- Willingness to accept failure

Qi
Free flow of internal energy

Promote Active Communication

Informal, Non-verbal, All Levels

Cultivate Positive Mental Attitudes

Succession, Image, Attitude, Rest/ Recreation

Fast

5.3 Managing with the Head and the Heart

➤ **Central to the Nursing Phase is the interplay between:**

   ✓ **Corporate Philosophy, and**
   ✓ **'qi', the Internal energy**

➤ **Corporate philosophy is oriented towards the Western concept (more direct), and acts on the head**

➤ **'qi' is oriented towards the Oriental concept (more indirect), and acts on the heart**

> Together they form the core beliefs that tell people what is sacred, what is sanctioned and what is taboo

> Supporting these core beliefs of Corporate philosophy and qi, other pre-requisites and qualities act like non-drug-based therapies for strengthening the physical immune system

  ✓ positive mental attitude
  ✓ active communication, and
  ✓ eating and exercising well

> Manage yourself, use your brain.
> Manage others, use your heart.

5.4 The 8 Steps to Building a Strong and Healthy Corporate Immune system

The 8-step prescription includes:

- ✓ Incorporating a New Corporate philosophy
- ✓ Strengthening the Free flow of Internal Energy
- ✓ Instilling a strong and healthy corporate culture
- ✓ Engendering Action-driven orientation
- ✓ Eating a balance diet
- ✓ Promoting active communication
- ✓ Cultivating a Positive mental attitude
- ✓ Emphasizing exercise

5.4.1 Incorporating a New Corporate Philosophy

The primary task here is to re-orient the entire company's mindset along the following fundamental tenets:

> ➤ New Ideas and ways of doing things

> ➤ Acceptance of Change as a constant

> ➤ Willingness to accept failure as a result

> The new and timeless corporate philosophy is like a drug which loses its efficacy when left on the shelf for too long.

New Ideas and Ways of doing things

- ➢ Ideas have become the chief raw material for companies to succeed in the new Knowledge economy

- ➢ Success stories based on New ideas abound in almost all industries today

  - ✓ Jesus' commissioning of his disciples from fishermen to 'fishers of men'

  - ✓ The alleged 'foolish' thinking of Walt Disney resulting in the greatest entertainer

✓ Merck's entering the healthcare industry with the acquisition of 'Medco'

✓ 3M's practice of 'boot-legging' resulting in innovations like 'post-it'

These are all examples of great Ideas – out-of-the-box thinking

> If what you are going to do is based only on what is already known, you cannot expect innovation.
>
> Masaru Ibuku

Acceptance of Change as a Constant

Organizations that outlast competitors stay nimble, springy and forward-looking *by living and breathing change*

Rapid obsolescence is the hallmark of today's turbulent world

To thrive you need to destroy, create, and rebuild with this process repeated several times if necessary

> We have to be willing to cannibalise what we're doing today in order to ensure our leadership in the future. It's counter to human nature but you have to kill your business while it is still working.
>
> **Lou Platt**

Willingness to accept Failure as a result

Today's business environments are fraught with many external viruses

The key to corporate success is to learn from our mistakes faster, and not to repeat them

Failure act as fertilizers in which subsequent successes are nurtured to full bloom

> No man ever achieved worthwhile success who did not, at one time or other, find himself with at least one foot hanging well over the brink of failure.
>
> **Napoleon Hill**

5.4.2 Strengthening the Free flow of Energy

➢ 'qi' (Internal Energy) is a concept central to Chinese medicine

➢ You can feel it, but cannot examine it under a microscope

➢ In the corporate Western context 'qi' is the human spirit, drive, passion and energy

➢ It is the relentless drive for progress – a drive that arises from human *urge to explore, create and improve*

➢ The interplay between corporate philosophy and 'qi' is what creates long-term success.

> You can have all the intelligence in the world, but if you don't have that desire or that passion to really, truly make it the very best, you will never be the very best.
>
> Roy Coleman

5.4.3 Instilling a Strong and Healthy Corporate Culture

➢ Corporate culture is collectively an ***internalized, deeply embedded set of beliefs, expectations and assumptions that influences and guides the thinking and behavior among organization members***

➢ It is distinct and exists in every organization

➢ A strong and healthy corporate culture is like a strong immune system helping the company to combat viruses

➤ Corporate culture embraces the concepts of:

- New corporate philosophy
- 'qi' or Internal energy
- Action-orientation by being flexible, fast and focused

➤ A weak corporate immune system can cause the downfall of a corporation as it is unable to cope with the changes in the marketplace

> **Natural forces within us are the true healers of disease.**
> **Hipprocrates**

5.4.4 Engendering Action-driven Orientation

➤ The three Fs of Action-driven orientation:

1. Flexibility in the corporate culture facilitating smooth adaptation to change
2. Fast and first in implementation of the right operational strategy
3. Focus on the areas of core competence

> Either you make history or you become history.
> **David Johnson**
>
> Companies must become turbo-marketers – be faster in product development, manufacture, distribution and service.
> **Philip Kotler**

5.4.5 Eating a Balanced Diet

➢ Ken Blanchard (author of *The One Minute Manager*) said, 20 years ago, that feedback is the breakfast of a champion

➢ Today you need:

Vision for breakfast
Feedback for lunch, and
Action for dinner

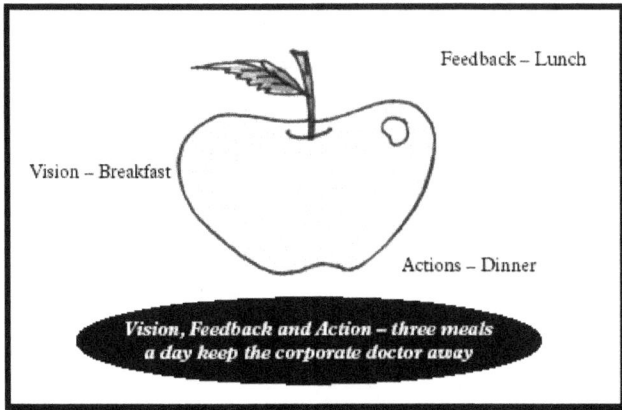

Vision – Breakfast
Feedback – Lunch
Actions – Dinner
Vision, Feedback and Action – three meals a day keep the corporate doctor away

5.4.6 Promoting Active Communication

➢ In Phase I – Surgery, Communication style tends to be close and didactic

➢ During the Nursing phase, the CEO needs to create a culture marked with candor and straight-talk

➢ Market information, and Ideas need to be speedily acted upon and exploited in order to fully harness their value

> In Phase III – Nursing, communication has to be more open and inter-active. It calls for:

  Informal and non-hierarchical structure

  Non-verbal communication

  Frequent communication at all levels

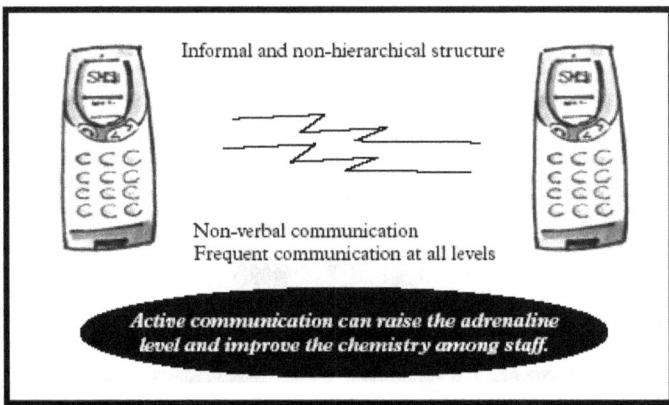

Informal and non-hierarchical structure

Non-verbal communication
Frequent communication at all levels

Active communication can raise the adrenaline level and improve the chemistry among staff.

5.4.7 Cultivating a Positive Mental Attitude

A positive mental attitude includes the following:

- Preparing for succession
- Enhancing professional image
- Improving Employee attitude
- Encouraging Rest and Recreation

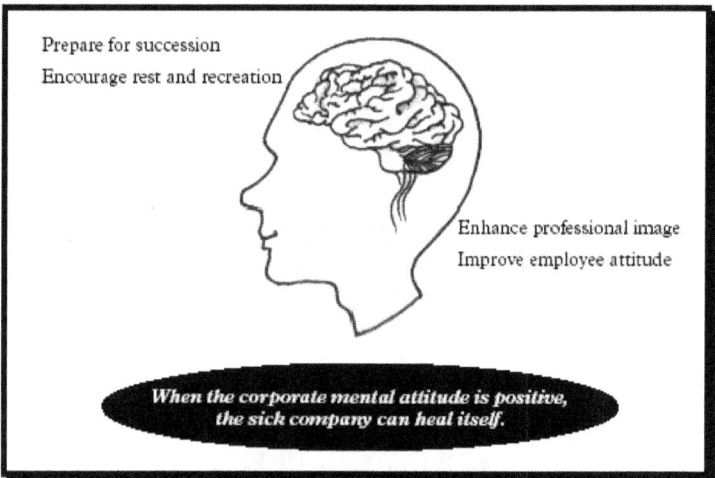

Prepare for succession
Encourage rest and recreation

Enhance professional image
Improve employee attitude

When the corporate mental attitude is positive, the sick company can heal itself.

5.4.8 Emphasise Exercising: Training and Development

Motivating employees through Training and Development has the following impacts:

- Pay Dividends in the long run
- Transform the mindset
- Engender a Quality Service culture
- Act as a catalyst for change

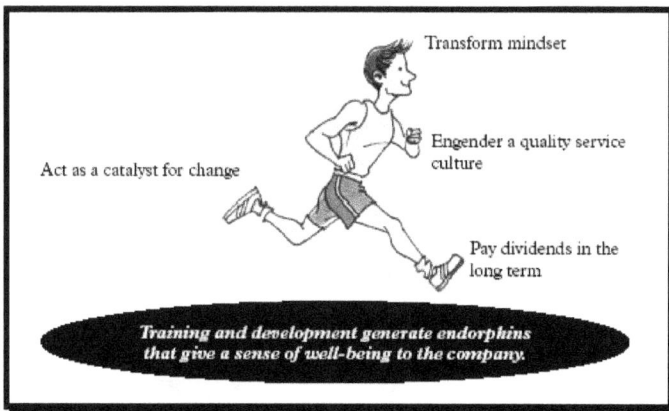

Transform mindset

Engender a quality service culture

Act as a catalyst for change

Pay dividends in the long term

Training and development generate endorphins that give a sense of well-being to the company.

Illustration

Capsules

On

Nursing Phase

Need for Creativity and innovation in Turnaround situations and in Healthy Companies

A key point that turnaround experts agree upon is that change is the best medicine for a sick or healthy company, and how a company obtains that change is through creativity. The standard tools we have described in this book need to be tuned to each user.

Jack Welch (GE) concludes that most innovations come from the suggestions and needs of the company's customers. It does not take a multi-million dollar research budget to develop them. And Thomas Edison, the inventor of the light bulb and a thousand other patents, advised that most innovations are found accidentally by working on something else. The key phrase is to have the flexibility to be working on something new.

In a recovery mode there is no better time to come up with something new—a new product or service. An example is in the present energy and environmental fields. Consider that thousands of new products will be needed in these fields.

Consider that this may be the time for your company to throw down the crutches of selling only commodity products and enter these fields. Products and companies come and go those that stay welcome expertise and change.

An example is Beijing, China today: According to *Breitbart News*, every monitoring station in Beijing's urban districts recorded levels of particulates seven times higher than the safety standard, according to the Beijing environmental protection bureau. People who are feeble, old or the young are advised to stay in their houses. China is recognizing they must make a turnaround about pollution. Where are the companies that can help China solve this problem? They will come, and probably some will be your competitors. Every problem has a challenge and alert and talented business companies have historically been known to solve it.

Do not rest upon your laurels – Shanghai Motor and other examples

The success of growth and not staying flat by Shanghai Automotive now puts them in an excellent position to move on the marketing front. A non-performing company often has to pass up such opportunities.

For example, China's own domestic market for their products is in rapid growth. They are now in a position to make that growth their growth. Their Chairman Hu Maoyuan indicated in 2006 that their goal for 2010 is to be manufacturing two million vehicles, with their own first hitting the streets in 2007. What will they do with all those vehicles, you ask? Well, in China today, the income is rising in many parts and there are estimated to be only 8 vehicles per one thousand of population, whereas in Japan, for example, the number is 502 vehicles per one thousand people.

And the don't-rest-upon-your-laurels example of Shanghai Automotive is true with many other companies in Asia such as Lenovo, Samsung, and Toyota. With overseas investment restrictions expected to be lifted in China, many companies in either growth or turnaround there will have an option of not only creating and borrowing, but also buying. From the cases to date it is clear that Chinese based and run companies, and perhaps most Asian companies, plan longer term growth compared to the West: centuries have taught the Chinese people to be patient and not be overly governed by the quarterly earnings crunch. In planning for a turnaround and recovery this factor is most important.

Need for Improvements even when you are successful - Toyota

The world sees Toyota Motor Corp., as an unstoppable profit company that may replace General Motors as the world's largest auto maker. But the CEO of Toyota is not resting on these trophies and laurels. He is known for his fierce insistence on efficiency, and just because his company is now in front, he does not let up with what has been his successful DNA drive for the company.

CEO Katsuaki Watanabe, has warned the Toyota may be losing its competitive edge around the world. He wonders if the company's factories are efficient enough. He has even questioned a core tenet of Toyota's culture—*kaizen, The Wall Street Journal—Asia Edition,* reported in December, 2006.

Taking what CEOs Mr. Wantanabe (Toyota) and Mr. Scaroni (Eni) believe and practice, the steps of turnaround are not patented tools of the very sick, but are used across the board in healthy as well as sick companies.

Change Management – Case of Optus Communications

A change management firm studied 21 of the most remarkable transformation stories of recent years and discovered in their report of 2002 that four principles underpinned the success of each one of those companies. Although the principles are easy to write they are not easy to achieve:

Set high standards and lead by example.

Put the right managers in place and give them real power.

Focus on results, not on an elaborate change process.

Do it quickly—tackle issues in parallel not in sequence.

What this study concluded conforms to other studies and when they advise that the implementation of these four points is not easy the examples of what is not easy can be: In order to put the right managers in place and give them real power it may take an entire change of management. Then keeping a clear view of the path the company must take is critical, and some incentives, such as small bonuses to the employees for outstanding performances are one of the better investments. An example cited is Continental Airlines that made a tough turnaround in difficult market and industry times. They provided employees incentives linked to short-term and clearly identified goals such as their

on-time bonus of $65 or $100 a month. The Bain study also indicated that the turnaround programs that work are usually completed in less than three years. One other company mentioned in the study notes was Optus Communications a telecommunications firm in Australia. In the late nineties the company faced problems of before-tax losses, cash squeezes, the end of Australia's telephone duopoly, and a revolving door to the CEO's office. The company came within an inch of liquidating.

Optus's successful turnaround started after they replaced the CEO and CFO and installed an entirely new management team for fresh blood, without the anchors of doing things the same as before or holding on to positions that needed revamped. They brought the cash flow shortage under control, and a number of other measures of efficiency then implemented a long delayed IPO. In 2001 it was purchased by Singapore Telecom for twice the IPO price.

Employee Motivation – Key to success – Virgin Airlines and Harley Davidson

When the amazing Richard Branson was interviewed on keys for success of Virgin Airlines, he replied: "I'm absolutely certain that it is a question of the kind of people you have; the way you motivate your people. I'm sure that is what makes a company successful. If you can motivate your people you can get through bad times, and you can enjoy the good times together. If you fail to motivate your people, your company is doomed not to perform well. I find I spend a lot of time trying to concentrate on motivating. Part of Virgin's management philosophy is based on the fundamental belief that the individual is all-important in our company."

If there is a any great secret of success in life

It lies in the ability to put one's self in another's place and see things from another's point of view

as if it were your own.

-Henry Ford

There are positive forces not shown on the balance or financial sheets of a company as well: The assets Mr. Branson referred to—the company employees.

When a company is sick, employees make the difference in success if they have leadership and a mission they believe in. Good employees, well motivated, have the ability to take a boomerang and flip it back: restoring the company through dedication and work. There are many examples of this. Harley-Davidson Motorcycle Company was facing bankruptcy just when motorcycles were becoming popular with different age groups again. The factory faced closure. Through the hard work of the company employees who were dedicated and motivated to keep the low throated Harley roaring on the streets of the world a restoration was begun. Employees worked long hours and many months without pay. Management communicated with them on a weekly basis, having personal picnics where the company made their work teamwork. And management mixed socially with the employees at their factory picnics, not through some third party such as E-mail, but face to face, handshake to handshake, and ear to ear. When the company finally made its turnaround, they did as Mr. Branson suggested: ". . . celebrate their success together." The "extra" that is so essential. And it doesn't appear anywhere on the financial papers that a company files.

People are the biggest assets

For an example of "what goes around comes around," the history of Sam Walton, the founder of Wal-Mart provides a picture. He took five hours at a shareholders meeting to individually thank his then four thousand excellent performing staff. Afterwards, he invited them all to his home.

In a short poll taken in 2006 of key production people listed companies, it was determined that none of these key personnel had ever met their CEO or upper management. If the CEO and management faced a deadly disease called low sales and low cash flow, would these workers be inclined to work without pay for people they had never met? Hardly.

There were some relevant findings made that illustrate the above point further: In 1978, on average, book value represented 95% of market value for a company, while 10 years later it was 28%. Today, it is estimated that 80% of stock value is driven from assets that do *not* (emphasis added) appear on balance sheets, assets like people, brands, knowledge, and relationships.

It is the wrong emphasis to place on a company, particularly when it is sick, to quack into the wind with strategies and resolutions when you do not have the right people doing the job. To make a turnaround and compete successfully people are needed to perform successfully on an internal company level.

People often marvel at Bill Gates, Jr. the founder of Microsoft and describe him as either rich or giving away a lot of his billions. He is described as impatient. He is that. But he is usually impatient with sloppiness. If the essentials of a meeting cannot be explained in thirty minutes or reduced to notes on a 3 X 5 card (inches)— he's gone. He is an example of innovation. He is an example for his employees many of whom are dedicated and passionate about the success of their company. When most heads were turned in the late seventies to designing the big iron of computing, he concentrated on the nervous system of computing—software. When the big opportunity came with IBM he was ready: "Let them do the hardware thing and I'll do the software," he must have thought.

But the other side of Bill's story is that money never was his motivation. He came from a family of considerable dedication to helping their fellow human beings—this was how he was raised and how he is now living his life. Mother, Mary, gave hours of her time and talent to education and solving the needs of those who were without. Bill's father was one of Seattle's finest lawyers and helped his community in many ways. When Bill became bored with college and cycled up the driveway, this is the kind of home he returned to. If his dear mother then said to her, "I don't know what is going to happen with that boy," no one would blame her. What goes around comes around. Gates, the younger, saw the big picture.

The myth of - If it runs don't fix it

Microsoft – Apple example

When a company needs a doctor, a turnaround expert, it has been found that in determining the diagnosis, the company products needs to be examined as well. It is not enough that the company has an established Research and Development centre within the company or via collaboration with another company: it may not be producing new and profitable products. It may be only protecting the products that have already slowed down in sales—the core products for the company in the past. A good example of this is Microsoft. They invest six billion dollars a year in Research and Development. But 90% of this investment is devoted to improving their existing core product Windows. As a result, its return on this investment is very poor.

But Apple did not sit on its laurels from the very successful launch of Mini iPod in 2005, their Research and Development centre kept working for new products and came up with the Nano iPod in 2006, which is an entirely new product—not just an improvement to their already successful core product. Nano iPod runs on a solid-state Flash memory instead of disk drive storage, allowing for a much smaller and more durable product.

This move was considered very risky by the technology media. It is, however, a good example of top leadership: Steve Jobs has been consistent in repeatedly pushing his employees to take risks rather than fall into complacency (trying to protect the successful Mini).

Xerox Example

Another example of the failure of executing on new products is Xerox: in the 1970s horse race of technology it was about as healthy a winner as a company can achieve. To continue their wins they set up a top notch R&D centre in California. This would normally be the right move if executed well. The purpose of the centre was to develop new products beyond the photocopier, and they did: the laser printer, the graphical interface, the mouse, and typography language among others. But none of these innovations entered the Xerox sales channels. Management was obviously still thinking copier thoughts. Other companies marketed those innovations: Canon and HP, the laser printers, Apple the graphics, and Adobe with typography. Blocking is not only a psychological condition it is also a corporate management malady. "If it runs, don't fix it" philosophy has stranded many a motorist on the road to success.

The Case of Turnaround of Japan as a country – Value systems

Turnaround examples are not always obvious and may come in different forms.

An excellent example is Japan during the decade of the nineties. And Japan's turnaround was clearly Japanese. Governments in turnarounds are helpful to study for all in the turnaround realm. Companies are micros of governments.

Japan's economy in 2006 is the world's second largest ($4.7 trillion) after the United States and one of the top three or four militaries.

In the 1980s and before Japan seemed to be immune to any economic sicknesses. In the 1990s the annual growth of 8% in the 80s fell just as fast as its terrific health had gained. Like a tsunami the state guided economy could not be stopped during a decade of stagnation since the late 1980s, suffering stock market and real estate crashes.

But since 2002 Japan has been on a rebounding turnaround. It has been concluded Japan's declining decade was not a sickness but a restructuring period. Japan companies halt the downfall began new programs: They sold subsidiaries that were expense holes, moved production abroad, and expanded merit based compensation.

The Japanese government played a role in the turnaround as well by modifying the pension system, revised corporate law, and removed a stack of bad loans. Then it reorganized itself as well.

They followed the German style of restructuring labour rather than that of the UK or the US which includes representatives of labour in the governance of the company. The plus side of this is strikes and labour disputes have been kept to a minimum and communication of the health of the company is more a part of a team effort throughout the entire company. Japanese companies have benefited from low turnover of employees. This is often a critical factor in a company's health. However, in the U.S. labor has few rights in the governance of the company and therefore labour is not integrated into the governance of the company. American corporations have nearly the right of complete freedom in hiring and firing employees. The result often is the only alternative labour has for change of policy on wages and benefits is a strike. However, what works for one culture may not for another. Although the labour laws of the U.S. have shifted over time with elections, the culture and voters have upheld the right of the companies to control their business and to generally keep the government out of business.

Japanese companies have also turned away from mergers and acquisitions to solve turnaround and growth problems. In the U.S. mergers and acquisitions make big headlines almost on a daily basis for the industrial news media such as the Wall Street Journal and other business publications. Company statements in Japan indicate that they see mergers and acquisition as disruptive and gimmicky.

And in supplier shopping for the lowest cost, the vice chairman of NEC has recently stated: "If you just procure what is the cheapest then what do you do about the cost of developing the next technology.

The concept of social harmony is a theme of the Japan turnaround and is valued because it provides a valued sense of harmony and develops a more long term value.

Section - 6

Conclusion

6.1 Parallels between Corporate Turnaround Phases and the Western-Eastern Medical Treatments

Medical Systems	Phase I Surgery	Phase II Resuscitation	Phase III Nursing
Medical Orientation	Western		Eastern
Medical Emphasis	Scientific – emphasising quick cure effects and hard issues.		Philosophic – emphasising preventive effects and soft issues.
Medicine	Chemical – having side-effects such as low morale after downsizing exercise.		Natural – having little side-effects as efforts are directed at winning the "heart" of the people.
Methodology	Analytic – step-by-step methodology is possible. More use of the "brain".		Comprehensive – less systematic and more experiential. More use of the "heart".
Clinical Difference	Local (partial) – focusing on improving cash flow, profits and sales. Tends to be financially-driven.		Holistic (wholeness) – giving importance to also other inter-related issues such as corporate culture, mindset and drive/passion. Tends to be people-driven.
Strengths/ Recommended Applications	Acute – addressing life and death cases and trauma care etc.		Chronic – addressing morale problem, negative mental attitude etc.
Diagnostic Approach	Clinical laboratory testing – results can be easily quantified and measured through financial and accounting system.		Human experience – results difficult to be quantified, more qualitative in nature.
Treatment Procedures	Standardised – applying an autocratic management style with little room for deviations.		Individualised – applying an empowerment and democratic management style, allowing room for deviations.
Treatment Objective	Reduction of symptoms – applying across-the-board cut in operating budgets to achieve the financial targets.		Elimination of the root cause- strengthening the corporate immune system to weather the uncertainties of the future.

6.2 A Comparative Summary of the Turnaround Phases

	Phase I: Surgery	Phase II Resuscitation	Phase III Nursing
Financial Emphasis	Cash Flow	Revenue/profits/ cash flow	Sustainable revenues/ profits/cash flow
Time-frame	Short – Few months	Medium – Less than 1 year	Long – More than 1 year
Corporate Orientation	Focus	Focus/Fast	Focus/Fast/ Flexible
Viral Treatment	Internal Viruses	Internal/ External Viruses	Internal/ External Viruses
Management Control	High – Autocratic	High/Medium – Democratic	Low – Empowerment
Leadership Style	Benevolent Dictator	Coaching Manager	Spiritual Leader
Communication Mode	Close/didactic	Didactic	Open/Interactive
Intensive Care Unit (ICU)	In ICU	Partially out of ICU	Out of ICU
Management Focus	Hard and "brain" issues	Hard and "brain" issues	Soft and "heart" issues

Cases

1. Turnaround of Continental Airlines

2. David Krall's Dilemma at Avid Technology

Turnaround of Continental Airlines

The remarkable turnaround strategy adopted and implemented by Gordon Bethune for revitalising Continental Airlines, one of the leading players in the US commercial airlines industry, is now a well known lesson for many corporate turnaround specialists. Once known as "The Proud Bird With The Golden Tail," Continental boasts a long and distinctive history that began on July 15, 1934 with single-engine Lockheed aircraft on dusty runways in the American Southwest.

In early 1994, Gordon Bethune had left his position in Boeing to take up the challenge in Continental Airlines. This case narrates the story of the Airline when Bethune joined, and details the strategy he planned and implemented to turn the Airline around.

The 8-year financial and operating summary figures, for the period from 1993 to 2000 are given in exhibit 1.

What was wrong in 1994

After having survivied a Chapter 11 Federal Bankruptcy filing for reorganization in 1983, Continantal Airlines was forced to go in for a second bankruptcy filing on December 3, 1990 due to rising fuel costs caused by the Iraqi invasion of Kuwait. During this time, Continental unveiled its Blue-and-Grey identity in Feb 1991, and went on to lauch the award-winning Business-First service in 1992 on transoceanic flights. In November 1992, Air Partners / Air Canada invested $450 million in Continental leading to the second bankruptcy emergence.

As can be seen from exhibit 1, Continental Airlines had clocked revenues of close to $5.8 billion in 1993 and 1994, but had reported net losses in both years. In fact, Continental had been in the red for over 5 years prior to 1993 as well. This had been despite the fact that Continental Airlines was ranked as the fifth largest commercial airline in the US in 1993, in terms of revenues. *Air Travel Consumer Report* is a magazine that reports statistics complied by the Department of Transportation in the US, and according to those reports, the following were the findings with respect to Continental in early 1993-94:

- In on-time arrivals (the percentage of flights that arrived within 15 minutes of the scheduled time) Continental was ranked last among the ten largest commercial airlines.

- Continental ranked highest amongst cases of mishandled baggage reports per 1,000 passengers

- It had the highest number of complaints per 100,000 passengers.

- Complaints filed with the DOT by Continental passengers were 30 percent higher than the ninth-ranking airline, and three times the industry average.

- Continental ranked among the worst in the percentage of passengers who were denied boarding passes because of overbooking and other problems.

Owing to these diverse operational problems, Continental also had to face frequent changes in top management, with as many as 10 CEOs having changed over the past 10 years. Employees had lived through several internal doses of surgery, resusciatation and attempts at nursing in the form of reorganizations, revitalization and turnaround efforts, and strategy shifts. Many employees were disillusioned, and morale was low, with signs of frequent infighting among departments.

Bethune himself was contemplating in terms of leaving Continental within four months of joining, considering the lack of support from the Board and the CEO. In late October 1994, to keep Bethune from leaving, Continental's board agreed to give him more authority. The Board told Bethune on October 24 that he could run the company for the next 10 days and would then be given an opportunity to present his plans for Continental's future.

Gordon Bethune's Go Forward Plan for Continental

Bethune's first act when he temporarily took over on October 24 was to prop open the doors to Continental's Executive suite, which previously had been locked and monitored by security cameras. He wanted people to enter freely at any time, and he wanted to begin to change the atmosphere in the Executive suite.

Next, he asked Greg Brenneman, a Bain & Company vice president with expertise in turning companies around, to help him draw up a Plan for Continental

Bethune and Breneman came up with what they called the **Go Forward Plan.** It had four parts –

- Fly to Win – the Market Plan

- Fund the Future – the Financial Plan

- Make Reliability a Reality – the Product Plan, and

- Working Together – the People Plan

Fly to Win

The guiding principle behind the market plan (Fly to Win) was for Continental to stop doing those things that were losing money or causing the company to lose money, and to concentrate on Continental's market strengths. They found, the company was losing money in 18% of its routes, many of which were low-fare point-to-point routes where it had a relatively low market share. On taking a hard look, they had found that 'Continental Lite' the company's low-fare/no-frills operation that was modeled after Southwest Airlines, was a major money loser. Fly to Win entailed making drastic cutbacks in Continental Lite flights, and to focus on hub-and-spoke operations rather than point-to-point routes. Some hubs like Greensboro were closed down, and several routes trimmed.

These changes resulted in over-capacity in terms of available seats, since Continental had ten different types of aircraft in its large jet fleet, including a number of the large Airbus 300s. Hence, Bethune and Brenneman proposed disposing of all the A300 planes in Continental's fleet, thereby removing the necessity of special parts inventory, special facilites and people, and special procedures. On the whole this improved Continental's load factor substantially over a period of time (See exhibits).

Several other special marketing campaigns were drawn up to woo back passengers and Travel Agents.

Fund the Future

In October 1994, Continental was strapped for cash and burdened by debt - it owed considerable amount of money on its aircraft fleet and it had a $2 billion debt hangover from the Chapter 11 proceedings in 1993. Bethune and Brenneman concluded that it was critical for the company to have a credible financial plan for making a profit in 1995. They put together a package of proposed changes involving renegotiation of aircraft lease payments, refinancing some of Continental's debt at lower interest rates, postponing some debt repayments, and raising fares on certain routes. These moves, they projected, held a realistic chance of generating a profit of $45 million in 1995 (a substantial improvement over the $200 million in losses that Continental would likely show for 1994) and would produce sufficient cash flows for Continental to avoid another financial crisis.

Making Reliability a Reality

The product plan part of Bethune's multifaceted Go Forward Plan -Make Reliability a Reality- aimed at quantum improvements in Continental's on-time performance, baggage handling, and overall flying experience-doing the very things that would please customers and make them inclined to fly Continental again. The centerpiece of Bethune's product plan was to focus employees' attention on on-time performance by rewarding them with a $65 bonus each month that Continental was in the top five U.S. airlines in percentage of flights arriving on-time-as measured and reported monthly by the U.S. Department of Transportation.

Working Together

Bethune believed that the most important component of the Go Forward Plan was to radically change Continental's corporate culture. He was convinced that a successful turnaround at

Continental hinged on getting Continental's employees working together and creating a positive work environment.

In preparing for the board meeting, Bethune and Brenneman ran their ideas about changing the corporate culture by Continental's chairman, coworkers they trusted, and by friends and family. At this juncture, the culture-changing effort was general and conceptual rather than a list of specific action proposals.

Meeting with the Board

After the presentation of the Go Forward Plan by Bethune in the second week of November 1994, the Board held closed-door meeting, and after some bickerings, the final decision of the Board to elect Bethune as the CEO was conveyed to him by the Chairman. Bethune was disappointed that the decision to accept his Plan and appoint him as CEO was not unanimous. However, he thanked the Board, and got cracking on implementing the Go Forward Plan.

Implementation and Execution of the Go Forward Plan, 1995-2000

A sample of the steps taken by Bethune after taking over as CEO can give us an insight into his style:

- As a fisrt step, he closed down Continental's maintenance operations in Los Angeles, since Continental was shifting its focus to its hubs in Newark, Houston, and Cleveland

- In May 1995, Bethune named Brennman as Continental's COO

- He instituted open house for employees on the last working day of each month. Employees were invited to tour the executive offices on the 20th floor, visit Bethune and other executives, and help themselves to food and drinks

- Casual-dress Fridays were instituted for all employees except those dealing directly with customers

- Once he gathered a few employees along with the manuals containing the Company's regulations and procedures, and had the employees set fire to the manuals. Word was sent to employees in the field that they were expected to use their best judgements and deal with issues.

- Bethune and his executives held meetings with employees at virtually every site in the company, to explain to them the rationale behind the Go Forward Plan.

- Travel agencies were treated as partners, and given better incentives on achievement of targets

- Bethune invited 100 high-mileage frequent flyers, along with spouses, to a party at his house, and all attendees were given a leather ticket case

- During 1996-2000 period, Continental expanded its code-sharing efforts, entering into agreements with such domestic carriers as Northwest Airlines, Air Canada, American Eagle, and Horizontal Airline, and such international carriers as Alitalia, Air France, and Air China. In late 2001, a code-sharing agreement with KLM was aslo concluded.

- A new Financial controller, Larr Kellner was brought in to improve financial systems and MIS

In terms of numbers, these efforts spoke for themselves during this period. Exhibit 2 lists the achievements by Continental Airlines during this period.

Continental Airlines in 2001

In Jaunary 2001, Continental Airlines was named Airline of the Year by *Air Transport World*, a leading aviation industry trade magazine. Continental had received the Airline of the Year award in 1996 as well, and thus became the first airline to receive such an award twice in a 5-year period.. In 2001, OAG, a division of Reed Business Information and publisher of *OAG Pocket Flight Guides* named Continental as Best Trans-Atlantic Airline and Best Airline based in North America; Continental was also honoured by OAG as having the best frequent flyer program. The marketing information firm J.D. Power and Associates had named Continental as tops in customer satisfaction for four of the past five years.

During the first six months of 2001, Continental reported revenues of $5.0 billion, up 3.3 % over the $4585 billion in revenues for the first six months of 2000; net earnings for the period were $51 million, down sharply from the $149 million in the first two quarters of 2000. Management attributed the lower earnings in 2001 to the sluggish U.S. and global economies.

The 9/11 terrorist attacks on the World Trade Center and the Pentagon further crippled airline operations world-wide, and partucluarly in North America. Bethune indicated that Continental expected to take in only half its normal revenues during the next several weeks, and that even if it cut costs by 20%, Continental would incur losses of $200 million per month.

The Federal Government's Rescue package was announced as a bailout to keep the U.S airline industry solvent until air travel rebounded. Continental received $212 million in cash immediatley, and was expected to receive an additional $212 million before the end of 2001. Exhibits 2-6 give various operational and financial performance parameters during these periods.

As the case ends in November 2001, Continental is suddenly in another crisis. The big issue is what does Bethune do now and can Continental come through the crisis in decent shape.

Questions for Discussion

1) Enumerate the symptoms of illness that Continental Airlines evinced in 1994 when Gordon Bethune joined as COO

2) What are the key characteristics of the turnaround actions taken by Gordon Bethune during the period from 1994 to mid-2001? How did he turn Continental from being one of the worst airlines in 1994 to being the best by mid-2001? Identify the Surgery, Resuscitation and Nursing stages during these 7 years.

3) Do you think the Go Forward Plan was entirely successful? On hindsight, what aspect of the Plan, if any, was wrong with the Go Forward Plan?

4) Assuming you were appointed as a Consultant to Continental Airlines in the Fall of 2001, what would be your recommendations to tide over the ills of reduced passenger traffic and the Company's rapid cash drain?

Exhibit 1 *Financial and Operating Summary, Continental Airlines, 1993-2000*

	2000	1999	1998	1997	1996	1995	1994	1993
Financial data (in billions, except for per share data)								
Operating revenues	$9,899	$8,639	$7,927	$7,194	$6,347	$5,825	$5,670	$5,767
Total operating expenses	9,215	8,039	7,226	6,478	5,822	5.440	5,681	5,786
Operating income	684	600	701	716	525	385	(11)	(19)
Net income	342	455	383	385	319	224	(613)	(39)[1]
Basic earnings per share	$5.62	$6.54	$6.34	$6.65	$5.7S.	$4.07	$(11.88)	$(1.17)[1]
Diluted earnings per share	$5.45	$6.20	$5.02	$4.99	$4.17	$3.37	$(11.88)	$(1.17)[1]
Operating data								
Revenue passengers (000's)	46,896	45,540	43,625	41,210	38,332	37,575	42,202	38,628
Revenue passenger miles (millions)[2]	64,161	60,022	53,910	47,906	41,914	40,023	41,588	42,324
Available seat miles (millions)[3]	86,100	81,946	74,727	67,576	61,515	61,006	65,861	67,011
Passenger load factor[4]	74.5%	73.2%	72.1%	70.9%	68.1%	65.6%	63.1%	63.2%
Breakeven passenger load factors[5]	66.3%	64.7%	61.6%	60.1%	(30.7%	60.8%	62.9%	63.3%
Passenger revenue per available								
seat mile (cents)	9.84¢	9.12¢	9.23¢	9.29¢	9.01¢	8.20¢	7.22¢	7.17¢
Operating cost per available								
seat mile	9.76¢	8.99¢	8.89~	9.04¢	8.75¢	8.36¢	8.76¢	7.90¢
Average price per gallon of fuel	86.69¢	47.31¢	46.83¢	62.91~	60.92¢	55.02¢	53.52¢	5926¢
Actual! aircraft in fleet at end of period	371	363	363	337	317	309	330	316
Average age of aircraft fleet (years)	8.0	8.4	11.6	14.3	14.3	n.a.	n.a.	n.a.

1 - Covers only the period April 28. 1993, through December 31,1993, after Continental emerged from Chapter 11 bankruptcy proceedings that began in 1990; results prior to April 28 are not meaningful due to recapitalization of company and other matters pertaining to the bankruptcy matters

2 The number of scheduled miles flown by revenue passengers.

3 The number of seats available for passengers multiplied by the number of scheduled miles those seats are flown.

4 Revenue passenger miles divided by available seat miles.

5 The percentage of seats that must be occupied by revenue passengers in order for the airline to break even on an income before income tax basis, excluding nonrecurring charges, non-operating items, and other special items.

Exhibit 2 – Achievements and accolades – 1995 to 2000

Source: www.continental.com

July 18, 1995

Continental announced the largest quarterly profit in its history.

August 1995 - November 1995

Continental placed number one in domestic baggage handling among the 10 largest U.S. air carriers on the Department of Transportation's monthly Air Travel Consumer Report for four consecutive months.

December 1995

Business Week Magazine named Continental the Best NYSE Stock for the year. Continental's Class B Common Stock had risen from a low of $6.50 per share in early January to a high of $47.50 in December.

December 1995

Continental closed out 1995 with the largest annual profit in its 61-year history ($224 million). In addition, for the fourth quarter of 1995, the airline ranked #1 in on-time performance, #1 in baggage** handling and #2 in the least complaints.

January 1996

Continental launched the 1996 Go Forward Plan designed to continue the momentum of one of the greatest corporate turnarounds of the 20th century.

June 1996

Received J.D. Power Award for Best Airline on flights of 500 miles or more.

January 1997

Named *Air Transport World* Airline of the Year for 1996.

May 1997

Became first airline ever to receive back-to-back J.D. Power Awards for Best Airline on Flights of 500 miles or more.

January 1998

Announced all-time record annual profit of $640 million for 1997. Announced plan to form a strategic global alliance with Northwest Airlines.

March 1998

Announced intention to purchase 15 Next Generation Boeing 737-900 aircraft, making Continental the largest carrier to add the aircraft to its fleet.

April 1998

National Airline Quality Rating ranked Continental as the most-improved airline for the second year in a row.

August 1998

Results of J.D. Power Customer Satisfaction Study ranked Continental highest in many critical categories despite overall second place ranking.

October 1998

Received first Boeing 777 aircraft and prepared for nonstop service to Tokyo from Newark and Houston.

December 21, 1998

Continental was named one of the "100 Best Companies to Work for in America" by FORTUNE magazine in a study conducted in conjunction with the Great Place to Work Institute of San Francisco.

December 29, 1998

Continental and Northwest begin code-sharing on 28 weekly international flights between the U.S. and Japan, and 21 weekly flights to Singapore, Bangkok, Thailand and Seoul, Korea.

January 20, 1999

Continental Airlines claimed seven awards in the "OAG Airline of the Year Awards," rating as the best U.S. airline in voting by frequent flyers who subscribe to OAG print and electronic travel information services.

January 21, 1999

Continental reported its 15th consecutive profitable quarter and ended the year on a high note. The company announced an all-time record annual pre-tax profit for 1998 of $770 million, exclusive of previously announced fleet charges. This was the fourth consecutive year of record pre-tax profits at Continental. The company posted fourth quarter 1998 net income of $66 million.

January 28, 1999

Continental Airlines' frequent flyer program, OnePass, swept the prestigious Freddie Awards, garnering five awards including top recognition for "Program of the Year" and "Best Elite-Level Program." During *Inside Flyer's* 11th Annual Freddie Awards ceremony, the OnePass program also was honored with the "Best Award" in recognition of its Business First international upgrades, as well as "Best Customer Service" and "Best Website" for 1998.

January 31, 1999

Launched daily nonstop service from Houston to Tokyo, Japan. This is the first nonstop flight from Houston to Asia.

March 2, 1999

Retired the last Boeing 747-200 and last Boeing 737-200. Continental removed the aircraft to make room for 60 more-efficient Boeing jets being put into service in 1999.

March 10, 1999

For the second year, Continental won the Gold Award as "Top Airline to North America" in the 1999 European Travel Awards, presented by *Travel Trade Gazette Europa*.

April 2, 1999

Completed a successful airborne Year 2000 (Y2K) test of its aircraft communications system. Continental was the first commercial airline to fly an aircraft in a simulated Y2K environment.

April 8, 1999

Gordon Bethune is named as one of the 50 best CEOs in America by *Worth* magazine. Gordon ranked sixth among the business executives.

April 15, 1999

Continental Airlines reported its 16th consecutive profitable quarter with a first quarter net income of $78 million ($1.03 diluted earnings per share), excluding non-recurring gains and charges.

May 11, 1999

Ranked as the nation's No. 1 major airline in customer satisfaction for long-distance (500 or more miles) flights in a study by *Frequent Flyer* magazine and J.D. Power and Associates.

May 28, 1999

Continental's Web site (www.continental.com) ranked No.1 in customer satisfaction and loyalty by NPD Online Research, a division of The NPD Group.

July 19, 1999

Continental reported its 17th consecutive profitable quarter with second quarter net income of $137 million.

August 1, 1999

Daily nonstop service between New York and Tel Aviv was launched by Continental.

October 4, 1999

Continental signs on as corporate sponsor for NYC2000, and announces plans to celebrate with a Peter Max-painted jumbo jet.

October 14, 1999

Continental Airlines ranked as the No. 2 most admired global airline by Fortune magazine in the publication's "World's Most Admired Companies" list, published in the October 11 issue.

October 14, 1999

Continental Airlines and America West Airlines became the first two U.S. airlines to implement interline e-Ticketing.

October 15, 1999

Continental Airlines Executive Vice President and Chief Financial Officer Larry Kellner was named winner of the 1999 CFO Excellence Award for Turnaround Management by CFO magazine and Arthur Andersen.

October 18, 1999

Continental Airlines reported its 18th consecutive profitable quarter with third quarter net income of $110 million ($1.56 basic and $1.53 diluted earnings per share).

December 13, 1999

The jet fleet of Continental becomes the youngest among the 10 largest US airlines, with an average jet fleet age of 7.4 years.

December 15, 1999

Continental Airlines implemented its Customer First program and fine-tuned customer service policies, established new functions and provided training to thousands of staff.

December 20, 1999

For the second year in a row, Continental Airlines was named one of the "100 Best Companies to Work For in America" by *FORTUNE* magazine in a study conducted in conjunction with the Great Place to Work Institute of San Francisco. Continental jumped to No. 23 on the list from last year's ranking at No. 40.

January 1, 2000

Continental successfully completes the Year 2000 rollover.

January 18, 2000

Continental Airlines reported fourth quarter net income of $33 million ($0.48 basic and $0.47 diluted earnings per share), exclusive of previously announced gains and charges.

January, 26, 2000

Continental won two awards at the 2000 OAG Airline of the Year Awards and was the only U.S. carrier to win an OAG award. Continental won Best Short Haul Executive/Business Class and Best Frequent Flyer Program.

January 27, 2000

Continental Airlines OnePass frequent flyer program garnered four of the top Freddie Awards, including "Program of the Year" and "Best Elite-Level Program," during *InsideFlyer's* 12th Annual Freddie Awards ceremony. The OnePass program also received the "Best Award" in recognition of its 25,000-mile reward from New York or Houston to Tokyo, as well as "Best Website" for 1999. Continental finished in the top three in every other category for which it was eligible.

February 17, 2000

Continental Airlines was named the No. 2 Most Admired U.S. Airline by *FORTUNE* magazine in its "America's Most Admired Companies" list, published in the Feb. 21, 2000, issue. Continental moved up one position from its No. 3 ranking in 1999.

April 20, 2000

Continental Airlines reported first quarter net income of $14 million ($0.21 basic and diluted earnings per share).

May 9, 2000

Continental Airlines was ranked as the nation's No. 1 airline in customer satisfaction for both short-distance and long-distance flights in an independent study conducted by *Frequent Flyer* magazine in conjunction with J.D. Power and Associates.

June 19, 2000

Continental Airlines Chairman and Chief Executive Officer Gordon Bethune called for relaxation of restrictions on foreign ownership of U.S. airlines as the aviation industry faced a potential new round of consolidation. Bethune also pressed Continental's case for entry into Heathrow.

July 18, 2000

Continental Airlines reported record quarterly diluted earnings per share of $2.46, before extraordinary charges. This marked the 21st consecutive profitable quarter and the highest diluted earnings per share in company history.

July 25, 2000

Continental Airlines signed new five-year employment agreements with the carrier. The agreements were signed with Chairman and Chief Executive Officer Gordon Bethune, President and Chief Operating Officer Greg Brenneman, Executive Vice President and Chief Financial Officer Larry Kellner, Executive Vice President - Operations C.D. McLean, and Executive Vice President and General Counsel Jeff Smisek.

August 30, 2000

Continental Airlines took delivery of its first Boeing 767-400ER (extended range) aircraft. It was piloted to Houston by the airline's chairman and CEO, Gordon Bethune, a licensed commercial jet pilot and aircraft mechanic.

September 12, 2000

Continental Airlines increased the size of its stock repurchase program by the amount of cash proceeds paid from and after Jan. 1, 2000 to the company from purchases of common stock by employees and other participants under the company's employee stock purchase and stock option plans. Since the beginning of the year, these amounts totaled approximately $80 million.

September 21, 2000

Continental Airlines ranked the No. 1 innovative user of information technology among all airlines, according to the recently released *InformationWeek* 500 list. The airline ranked No. 25 out of 500 companies on the 12th annual list, coming in first among all carriers.

September 26, 2000

Continental Airlines was named the top U.S.-based global carrier in *Fortune* magazine's "World's Most Admired Companies" list. Continental ranked No. 3 overall in the Global Most Admired Airlines category published in the October 2 issue.

October 6, 2000

Continental Airlines' Executive Vice President and Chief Financial Officer Larry Kellner was awarded the 2000 CFO Excellence Award in the Information/Knowledge Management category, making him the first three-time winner in the history of the awards, sponsored by *CFO* magazine and Arthur Andersen.

October 11, 2000

Continental Airlines and Northwest Airlines launched the world's largest interline eTicket network.

October 16, 2000

Continental Airlines reported third quarter diluted earnings per share of $2.24 (before an extraordinary charge) a 56 percent increase over the same period in 1999. This marked the 22nd consecutive profitable quarter for Continental, and the highest third quarter earnings per share in company history.

November 6, 2000

Continental Airlines announced that it priced $250 million of convertible preferred securities of an affiliated special purpose trust, convertible into Continental Class B common stock maturing in 2030. The securities will pay cash distributions at an annual rate of 6 percent of their $50 per security liquidation amount, and will be convertible at the initial rate of 0.8333 shares of common stock for each security (equivalent to an initial conversion price of $60 per share of common stock). The Company granted the initial purchasers a 30-day over allotment option on an additional $37.5 million of the securities on the same terms.

November 10, 2000

Continental Airlines took delivery of its first 767-200ER aircraft.

November 16, 2000

Continental Airlines and Northwest Airlines executed definitive agreements regarding the sale to Continental of its common stock held by Northwest Airlines, and an extension of their alliance agreement through 2025. The boards of both airlines approved the agreements prior to their execution.

December 18, 2000

For the third year in a row, Continental Airlines was named one of the "100 Best Companies to Work For" by FORTUNE magazine in a study conducted in conjunction with the Great Place to Work Institute of San Francisco. Continental jumped to No. 18 on the list from last year's ranking at No. 23.

Exhibit 3 *Continental's Aircraft Fleet, June 30, 2001*

Aircraft Type	Total Seats	Aircraft Owned	Aircraft Leased	Total Aircraft	Average Age*	Aircraft on Order
Continental						
Boeing 777-200	283	4	12	16	1.7	2
Boeing 767-400ER	235	3	2	5	0.2	19
Boeing 767-200ER	174	7	1	8	0.1	2
Boeing 757-300	210	—	—	—	—	15
Boeing 757-200	172	13	28	41	3.9	—
Boeing 737-900	167	—	1	1	0.1	14
Boeing 737-800	155	17	43	60	1.3	33
Boeing 737-700	124	12	24	36	2.0	5
Boeing 737-500	104	15	51	66	4.7	—
Boeing 737-300	124	14	51	65	13.4	—
DC10-30	242	3	11	14	25.5	—
MD-80	141	17	48	65	15.9	—
		105	272	377		90
Continental Express						
Jets						
Embraer ERJ-145XR	50	—	—	—	—	75
Embraer ERJ-145	50	18	72	90	1.9	59
Embraer ERJ-135	37	—	27	27	0.7	23
Total jets		18	99	117		157
Turboprops						
ATR-42-320	46	9	22	31	10.8	—
EMB-120	30	9	10	19	11.0	—
Beech 1900-D	19	—	13	13	4.8	—
Total turboprops		18	45	63		—
Total		141	416	557		247

Note: Continental anticipated taking delivery of 36 Boeing aircraft in 2001 (of which 9 were placed in service in the first half of 2001. Continental Express anticipated taking delivery of 41 Embraer regional jets in 2001 (of which 21 were placed in service in the first half of 2001). Continental planned to retire 14 of its turboprop aircraft during the second half of 2001. As of June 30, 2001, Continental's estimated costs for the Boeing aircraft it had on order totaled $4.2 billion; its commitment for Embraer regional jet aircraft was approximately $2.5 billion. As of June 30, 2001, Continental had approximately $1.3 billion in financing arranged for future deliveries of Boeing aircraft.

Source: Continental Airlines, 2000 10-K report and 10-Q report, July 2001.

Exhibit 4 Continental's Passenger Load Factors, September 2001

	Sept 1-10	Sept 11-16	Sept 17-23	Sept 23-30
Continental				
Domestic	70.0%	58.0%	46.6%	58.5%
International	76.2	66.6	55.8	47.7
	----------	----------	----------	----------
Total	72.4	62.2	50.4	54.1
Continental Express	61.9	41.1	39.0	53.4

Source: Company records

Exhibit 5   Continental's Balance Sheet, September 30, 2001, versus December 31, 2000 (in billions of dollars)

	September 30, 2001	December 31, 2000
Assets		
Current Assets		
Cash and Cash Equivalents	$1,201	$1,371
Short-term Investments	---	24
Accounts receivables, net	455	495
Spare parts and Supplies, net	290	280
Other	306	289
Total Current Assets	2,252	2,459
Total property and equipment	6,603	5,163
Routes, Gates and Slots, net	1,048	1,081
Other Assets, net	453	498
	-------------	-------------
Total Assets	$9,816	$9,201
	===========	==========
Liabilities and Stockholders' Equity		
Current Liabilities		
Current maturities of long-term debts	$ 349	$ 304
Accounts payables	988	1,016
Air Traffic liability	1,124	1,125
Accrued other liabilities	623	535
Total Current Liabilities	3,084	2,980
Long-term debt and Capital Leases	4,092	3,374
Other long-term liabilities	1,145	995
Convertible Debentures	243	242
Redeemable Common Stock	----	----
Stockholders' Equity		
Preferred Stock	----	----
Class A Common Stock	----	----
Class B Common Stock	1	1
Additional paid-in capital	885	379
Retained Earnings	1,510	1,456
Accumulated other Comprehensive Income (loss)	(4)	13
Treasury stock	(1,140)	(689)
Total Stockholders' Equity	1,252	1,160
	-------------	-------------
Total Liabilities and Stockholders' Equity	$9,816	$9,201
	===========	===========

Source: Company news release, October 31, 2001

Exhibit 6 *Selected Operating Statistics for Continental Airlines, Three Months Ending September 30, 2001; versus 2000 (figures do not include Continental Express operations)*

	Three Months Ended September 30		Net Increase (Decrease)
	2001	2000	
Revenue passengers (000s)	11,254	12,155	(7.4)%
Revenue passenger miles [1]	16,206	17,325	(6,5)%
Available seat miles (millions)[2]	21,994	22,356	(1,6)%
Passenger load factor[3]	73.7%	77,5%	(3,8) points
Break-even passenger load factor[4]	78.3%	67.4%	10,9 points
Passenger revenue per available seat mile	8.59¢	10.06¢	(14.6)%
Total revenue per available seat	9.33¢	10.89¢	(14,3)%
Operating cost per available seat	9.34¢	9.58¢	(2.0)%
Average price per gallon of fuel	82.37¢	86.52¢	(4.8)%
Actual aircraft in fleet at end of	342	367	*(6.8)°/0*
Average length of aircraft flight	1,208	1,187	1.8%

1 The number of scheduled miles flown by revenue passengers.
2 The number of seats available for passengers multiplied by the number of scheduled miles those seats is flown.
3 Revenue passenger miles divided by available seat miles.
4 The percentage of seats that must be occupied by revenue passengers in order for the airline to break even on an income before income tax basis, excluding nonrecurring charges, non-operating items, and other special items.

Source: Company news release, October 31, 2001.

David Krall's Dilemma at Avid Technology

If you enjoy movies, television, music, videogames, or virtually any other form of electronic media, you have almost certainly experienced the work of the legions of content creators who use Avid solutions to bring their creative visions to life. This case narrates the story of Avid Technology, Inc. around early 2000, when David Krall was elevated to the position of CEO, with complete responsibility for turning around the Company.

Avid Technology Inc. was founded in 1987 by William J Warner, who left his position at Apollo Computer Inc., a manufacturer of computer systems, to pursue his revolutionary idea of digitizing moving pictures and sounds so that they could be edited by computer. He started operations in a garage in Burlington, MA. Joining Warner in 1988 were Curt Rawley, a former president of Racal Design Services, a designer of printed circuit boards, and Eric Peters, a former engineer at Apollo Computer and Digital Equipment Corporation.

The three entrepreneurs developed Media Composer, the product upon which the new company was launched. Product shipments began in the fourth quarter of 1989. Sales grew rapidly, rising from $1 million in 1989 to $407million in 1995. Subsequently the sales growth dropped as shown below:

Year	Gross Revenues in $ million	% Increase
1989	1.0	
1990	7.4	640
1991	32.3	336
1992	69.0	114
1993	134.4	95
1994	233.6	74
1995	406.7	74
1996	429.0	5.5
1997	471.3	9.9
1998	482.4	2.4
1999	452.6	-6.2
2000	476.1	5.2

Source: Company website www.avid.com

To finance the company's rapid growth, Avid went public in 1993 (NASDAQ: AVID), generating additional capital of $53 million. In the same year, sales more than doubled, to $135 million. The company rose to the fifth position in *Inc.* magazine's list of "100 Fastest Growing Small Public U.S. Companies", and ranked ninth on *Fortune's* list of "100 Fastest Growing American Companies". Rapid growth continued, with Avid recording revenues of $234 million in 1994 and $407 million in 1995.

Through 1995, Avid was achieving its objectives to quickly gain market share and develop a leadership position in its markets. However, sales growth following 1995 slowed, with revenues increasing by only 5.5%, to $429 million in 1996; 10%, to $471 million in 1997, and 2%, to $482 million in 1998. In 1999, revenue decreased for the first time in the company's history, dropping 6%, to $453 million. Exhibit 1 provides a consolidated statement of operrations, and Exhibit 2 shows thw Balance sheet of the company. By the end of 1999, Avid had about 1,700 employees.

A key factor in Avid's rapid sales growth was its ability to establish a channel for international sales during its earliest days. Avid established sales offices in 7 countries by 1993, and by 1999 it had sales offices in 20 different countries. Exports grew very quickly from 11% of revenues in 1990, to 42% in 1992, and to 51% in 1999, with Avid selling to over 75 foreign markets. Exhibit 5 gives a snapshot of the various achievements by Avid till 2000.

Avid Markets and Products

Avid served three markets. The primary revenue source for Avid was the Film, Television and related industries, which was an early adopter of digital technology, and Avid was considered a clear leader in this market. Exhibit 3 provides a sample listing of films and TV programs created using Avid products. While the $1 billion Film industry was an early adopter, the $2 billion Television industry was still using tape-based analog technology, as was the $900 million audio industry. The $985 million corporate and institutional video industry was also prdominantly tape-based.

Avid's second most important revenue source was the $350 million news broadcast industry. Although the company had focused on this market since 1993, its efforts were less successful here, largely because Avid did not offer products that could perform all the functions in the processes of news broadcst creation.

The retail consumer market – buyers of editing products to create home videos and photos - was the third source of revenue for Avid. Avid competed in this market with 'Avid Cinema' with which special effects could be added to video recordings of school plays, weddings, birthday parties etc..

Avid's products could be classified into six categories: video and film editing products, audio products, digital news gathering systems, newsroom computer systems, graphics and special effects products, and storage systems. Avid's first product, Media Composer was an instant success and accounted for the rapid growth in the initial years. The company maintained a consistent level of R&D activity approximating 17% of sales, which mirrored the industry average. In addition, Avid engaged in several acquisitions to gain leading technology that the company believed complemented its existing in-house technology (See Exhibit 4). As a pioneer in digital technology, Avid took the lead in developing and promoting open industry standards, with its platform known as Open Media Framework (OMF), which grew, over a period of time, into a cooperative effort involving more than 150 leading manufacturers of digital products.

Avid Management

From its founding in 1989 through 1995, Avid's cofounders sequentially held the position of CEO. Warner was CEO till 1991, when he left to start another noncompeting company. Subsequently it was Curt Rawley till 1995.They both answered to a Board of Directors chaired by the general partner of Greylock Management Corporation, a venture capital firm that played a significant role in the company's initial equity funding.

In spite of such rapid growth and success till 1995, Avid's initial objectives to gain market share and develop a position of industry leadership eventually took their toll on company profitability. The Board decided that the emphasis needed to be shifted from being driven by market share to seeking balanced growth with increased profitability, and also concluded that the Company needed an 'outside' individual with experience running a large technology outfit.

In 1996, Bill Miller, 53, a seasoned executive in the technology industry, was hired to turn the fortunes of Avid around. Miller got into action very quickly and hired a new CFO to establish necessary financial control systems to decrease costs. Inventories and accounts receivable were significantly reduced from $63.4 million and $107.9 million, respectively, in 1995, to $9.8 million and $79.8 million in 1997. In an effort to boost the company's growth and profitability, Miller made significant changes to the distribution channels, concentrating on independent distributors, Value-Added-Rsellers, and dealers. Sales through indirect channel members grew from 50% in 1996 to 85% in 1999.

Miller also took his most significant strategic action of acquiring Softimage in 1998. Softimage was a leading developer of 3D animation, video production and compositing software, and hence was seen as broadening the product lines of Avid. But soon this became more difficult for Avid to digest than was expected. Three years into Miller's tenure as Avid's CEO, sales growth and profits remained elusive. In 1999, Avid recorded revenue of $452.6 million (a 6% decrease from 1998), and a net loss of $137.5 million – the company's worst performance in its 10-year history.

This resulted in the Board once again taking action towards restructuring to position the company for future growth and profitability.

David Krall appointed as CEO

David Krall, who was COO of Avid'd Digidesign division, was appointed to the position of CEO in April 2000. The Digidesign Division had been a bright spot for Avid; it had achieved record sales and operating income while the company as a whole was performing below expectations. Krall, 39, though a relatively young man with just 4 years experience in Avid, had a history as an innovator. He had won Harvard Business School's Entrepreneur of the Year Award for an invention he patented (a backup battery for laptop computers). His strong technical background, with BS and MS degrees from MIT and an MBA from Harvard, as well as his company and industry knowledge were expected to come to bear on the strategic decisions he would have to make to turn Avid around.

Krall and the new management team he needed to build, faced many challenges. The slow rate of growth and the staggering losses were of prime concern. Some industry analysts viewed the purchase of Softimage with skepticism, wondering if the sheer magnitude of the first cross-border acquisition by Avid was a trifle too much to digest. Besides the immediate need to bring expenses in line with revenues, the second concern in Krall's mind was laying the foundation for growth in the future. Meanwhile, Avid risked competition from international firms like Sony and Panasonic, that were attracted to the opportunities offered by the digital technologies the company had pioneered.

During his first year as CEO, Krall announced a new focus on Internet-related editing products and once again set Avid on an acquisition spree. In 2000, Avid purchased Pluto Technologies International and The Motion Factory for an aggregate of $2.3 million. Krall also oversaw an alliance with Intel and Microsoft to develop products for creating interactive digital television. Krall finishe dhis first year on a modestly successful note. Avid's 2000 revenues were up 5% from 1999, and although the company incurred a net loss of $56 million, it was significantly lower than the $137 million in 1999.

As Avid entered 2001, Krall knew he had to act fast. Krall had to assess whether he had addressed the causes of the company's past performance problems. In a ligher vein, going by Avid's history, it has roughly had a new CEO every three years, which meant, Krall had two years left to prove his mettle.

Questions for Discussion

1) What is your assessment of Avid Technology's financial condition when David Krall took over? Are there clear indications of failing health over a period of time? Substantiate your answers with numbers from the case.

2) What steps taken by David Krall pertain to the Surgery phase of corporate turnaround?

3) Discuss and evaluate the Blood Transfusion techniques used by Avid management before and under David Krall. In your opinion, was the Softimage acquisition the right treatment for Avid?

4) As a turnaround consultant to Avid Technology, what recommendations will you make to David Krall?

Exhibit 1- Avid Technology's Consolidated Statement of Operations, 1989-2000 (in millions except per share data)

	1989	1990	1991	1992	1993	1994	1995	1996	1997	1998	1999	2000
Net Revenues	0.9	7.4	20.1	51.9	112.9	203.7	406.6	429.0	471.3	482.4	452.6	476.0
Cost of Sales	0.5	3.4	9.6	23.7	54.1	99.9	198.8	238.8	221.5	190.2	205.9	234.4
Gross Profit	0.4	4.0	10.5	28.2	58.8	103.8	207.8	190.2	249.8	292.2	246.7	241.6
Operating Expenses	2.1	6.3	10.5	24.7	55.7	87.0	185.2	220.5	219.7	242.6	246.9	229.8
Non recurring costs	0	0.6	1.0	0.9	0	0	5.5	29.0	0	28.4	14.5	0
Amortization of acquired assets	0	0	0	0	0	0	0	0	0	34.2	79.9	66.9
Other Income (Expenses)	0	0.1	0.1	0	1.5	1.0	1.4	3.4	8.1	8.6	3.5	3.7
Income Taxes	0	0	0	1.2	0.9	4.8	8.6	(17.9)	11.8	(0.8)	46.4	5.0
	-----	-----	-----	-----	-----	-----	-----	-----	-----	-----	-----	-----
Net Income (Loss)	(1.7)	(2.8)	(0.9)	1.4	5.5	13.0	15.4	(38.0)	26.4	(3.6)	(137.5)	(56.4)
Net EPS	(0.57)	(0.84)	(0.27)	0.29	0.38	1.10	0.77	(1.80)	1.08	(0.15)	(5.75)	(2.28)
Common Stock Value												
High	n/a	n/a	n/a	n/a	27.16	43.50	48.75	25.88	38.00	47.75	34.25	24.50
Low	n/a	n/a	n/a	n/a	16.00	20.50	16.75	10.13	9.00	11.08	10.00	9.38

Notes: Non recurring costs primarily relate to write-offs resulting from restructurings and/or acquisitions
Amortization of acquired assets relates to the Softimage acquisition

Source: Avid Annual Reports and 10Ks 1989-2000

Exhibit - 2

Avid Technology's Consolidated Balance Sheet, 1998-2000 (in millions)

	1998	1999	2000
Assets			
Cash and marketable securities	$111.8	$72.8	$83.2
Accounts receivable, net	89.8	76.2	90.0
Inventories	11.1	15.0	21.1
Other current assets	29.0	12.6	11.7
Total current assets	241.7	176.4	206.1
Property, plant, and equipment, net	35.4	32.7	26.1
Other assets	209.6	102.9	34.2
Total assets	$486.7	$312.0	$266.4
Liabilities and Stockholders' Equity			
Accounts payable	$24.3	$24.0	$28.8
Other accrued charges	75.4	61.8	56.2
Deferred revenues	22.9	20.3	24.5
Total current liabilities	122.6	106.1	109.5
Long-term debt	13.3	14.2	13.4
Other	60.5	23.8	5.7
Stockholders' equity			
Common stock	0.3	0.3	0.3
Additional paid-in-capital	349.3	366.6	359.1
Retained earnings	14.3	(128.1)	(197.8)
Treasury stock	(68.0)	(66.5)	(15.6)
Deferred compensation	(3.8)	(1.9)	(4.8)
Cumulative translation adjustment	(1.8)	(2.5)	(3.4)
Total stockholders' equity	290.3	167.9	137.6
Total liabilities and stockholders' equity	$486.7	$312.0	$266.4

Source: Avid annual reports and 10Ks, 1998-2000

Exhibit - 3 Films and Television Programs Created Using Avid Products (Sample listing only)

Films	Television Programs
Lethal Weapon 4	*Ally McBeal*
Lost in Space	*Frasier*
The Perfect Storm	*Friends*
Star Trek: Insurrection	*Just Shoot Me*
Titanic	*Survivor II*
The X-Files: Fight the Future	*Veronica's Closet*

Note: 85 percent of films made in the United States in 2000 were edited on Avid systems, and 95 percent of prime time television programs in 2000 were edited on Avid systems.
Source: Avid Technology, Inc. public documents; The Boston Globe, April 30, 2001

Exhibit - 4 Significant Avid Acquisitions, 1993-2000

Year	Company	Revenues (in millions)	Cost (in millions	Description
1993	Digital Video Applications Corporation	n/a	$4.6	Developed video editing and presentation software products targeted for sale. to nonprofessional video editors
1994	Basys Automation Systems (newsroom division)	$26	$5	Developed Newsroom automation systems
	Softech Systems			Developed newsroom automation software
1995	Digidesign, Inc	$39	$205	Leading provider of computer-based digital audio production systems for the professional music, film, broadcast, multimedia and home recording markets
	Elastic Reality	$12	$45	Developed digital image manipulation software
	Parallax Software			Developed paint and compositing software
1998	Softimage	$37	$248	Leading developer of 3D animation, video production, 2D cel animation, and compositing software
2000	The Motion Factory	n/a	$2.3	Developed 3D media for games and the web
	Pluto Technologies International			Developed newsroom storage and networking products

Note:
1. Digital Video Applications Corporation was acquired to give Avid a presence in the nonprofessional video market as well as enhance its existing market capabilities.
2. Basys Automation Systems (newsroom division) and Softech Systems were acquired to provide Avid access to the news broadcast industry.
3. Digidesign, Inc. was acquired to give Avid a leadership position in the digital audio market.
4. Elastic Reality and Parallax Software were acquired to form Avid's graphics and effects group; the companies developed a range of image manipulation products that allow users in the video and film post-production and broadcast markets to create graphics and special effects for use in feature films, television programs and advertising, and news programs. The Softimage acquisition significantly strengthened Avid's capabilities and market presence in these areas.
5. The Motion Picture Factory was acquired to enhance Avid's gaming and Web capabilities.
6. Pluto Technologies International was acquired to diversify Avid's product offerings for the news broadcast industry.

Source: Avid annual reports, public documents, and on-site interview with company representative; Computer Reseller News, October 31, 1994; Newsbytes News Network), March 31, 1995; *Boston Herald*, October 22, 1998, and June 30, 2000; and CCN Disclosure, September 10, 2000

Exhibit -5 Snapshot of Avid Technology's achievements till 2000

1987

Avid Technology, Inc. is founded by William J. Warner in a garage in Burlington, MA.

1989

Avid introduces the industry to digital nonlinear editing with the Avid/1 Media Composer system, the company's flagship editing solution. The Media Composer system revolutionizes the postproduction process by providing editors with a faster, more intuitive, and more creative way to work than was possible with traditional analog linear methods. This development helps pave the way for a digital revolution within the film, video, and broadcast industries.
Avid posts revenue of $1 million.

1990

Avid opens its first office in Europe.

1992

Avid opens its first office in Asia.
Avid sells its 500th Avid/1 Media Composer system.
Avid introduces the Film Composer system, the industry's first digital nonlinear editing system that supports 24p.

1993

Avid goes public, trading on the NASDAQ market under the symbol AVID.
The National Academy of Television Arts & Sciences presents Avid with two Emmy Awards for the Media Composer system.
Neil Simon's *Lost in Yonkers* becomes the first feature film cut on the Avid Film Composer system.

1994

Avid acquires BASYS Automation Systems (news division) and SofTECH Systems, Inc., two leading providers of newsroom computer systems for broadcasters.
Avid introduces the Open Media Framework (OMF) interchange, an industry-standard file format for the exchange of digital media among different platforms and applications, and now widely recognized as a key enabling technology for all-digital postproduction.

1995

Avid acquires Digidesign, Inc., a pioneering developer of digital audio production solutions, including the Pro Tools digital audio workstation platform.
Avid acquires Parallax Software, Inc. and Elastic Reality, Inc., leaders in paint, compositing, effects, and image manipulation software.
Avid moves from Burlington to its current headquarters in Tewksbury, MA.

1997

Avid enters into strategic alliances with Intel and Matsushita to support its development plans on the Windows platform.
Cut on an Avid Film Composer system, *The English Patient* becomes the first digitally edited film to receive an Academy Award in the Best Film Editing category.

1998

Avid acquires Softimage, Inc., a Montreal-based developer of software tools for digital artists who create professional animation and visual effects for the film, broadcast, and games industries.
Avid receives an Emmy Award recognizing the real-time multicamera grouping option in the Media Composer and Film Composer digital editing systems.

1999

Avid receives an Oscar statuette representing the 1998 Scientific and Technical Award for the concept, design, and engineering of the Avid Film Composer system for motion picture editing.
David Krall joins Avid as chief operating officer, following a four-year tenure at Digidesign, where he also held the position of COO.

2000

Krall promoted to president and chief executive officer of Avid.
Avid receives an Emmy Award recognizing outstanding achievement in technological advancement for broadcast-quality PC video and compression plug-in cards.
Avid acquires The Motion Factory, Inc. of Fremont, CA, a company specializing in applications for the creation, delivery, and playback of interactive, rich 3D media for character-driven games and the Internet.
Avid acquires Pluto Technologies International, Inc. of Boulder, CO, a provider of video storage and networking solutions for broadcast news, postproduction, and other bandwidth-intensive applications.

Source: Company website www.avid.com

Suggested Solutions to the Case Questions

Needless to say, in a case study, we are always open to new ideas and interpretation coming from the delegates, and hence there are obviously no absolutely correct or wrong answers. The suggested answers given below are indicative of the points that are expected to be analysed by the delegates / participants during the case discussion.

Question 1
Enumerate the symptoms of illness that Continental Airlines evinced in 1994 when Gordon Bethune joined as COO

This question is intended to provoke some reflective thinking and perspective analysis on the part of the delegates / class members. Particularly, it sets the tone for applying what they have learnt during the introductory session on Medical analogies, and on that basis immediately come up with the specific symptoms that indicate that Continental Airlines is suffering from some major illness in 1994.

Typical responses should include, among others:

- Continental was literally **struggling for survival** in 1994
- In spite of being the fifth largest commercial airline with revenues close to $6 billion, the company had reported **net losses every year since 1985**
- In terms of **operating performance and customer satisfaction**, Continental **ranked last among the 10** major U.S. commercial airlines
- It was **last** among the top 10 airlines **in on-time arrivals**
- It had the **highest number of mishandled baggage reports** per 1,000 passengers
- By far the **highest number of complaints per 100,000 passengers**, with customer complaints about various aspects of their experience with Continental being **30% higher than the 9th** ranking airline, and **3 times the industry average**
- Ranked among the worst in percentage of **passengers denied boarding because of overbooking** and other problems
- 10 different CEOs in 10 years
- Employee disillusionment and low morale
- Turnover and use of sick time were very high
- On-the-job injuries were far above industry average
- Considerable infighting among employee groups and departments
- Continental's ticket agents and gate personnel had to deal with dissatisfied and angry passengers

It is important to ensure that, at this stage the participants enumerate only the symptoms, and do not come up with possible reasons for those symptoms!! After enumerating the symptoms, the discussion may proceed on diagnosis of the illness itself, leading up to the next question on what strategy Gordon Bethune used, and how the parallels with Surgery, Resuscitation and Nursing can be drawn.

Question 2
<u>**What are the key characteristics of the turnaround actions taken by Gordon Bethune during the period from 1994 to mid-2001? How did he turn Continental from being one of the worst airlines in 1994 to being the best by mid-2001? Identify the Surgery, Resuscitation and Nursing stages during these 7 years.**</u>

This is an excellent opportunity for the participants to bring out the phases of corporate turnaround, and highlight:

   a) The 4C's of Restructuring during the surgery phase
   b) The 8 pillars for Revitalising a business as part of the Resuscitation phase, and
   c) The 8 steps to building a strong and healthy corporate immune system as part of Nursing

in relation to Gordon Bethune's style and competence. Typical responses here should include:

- Bethune's diagnosis of the operating problems was excellent, and he also knew how to deal with each of them
- Bethune is a man of action and a person who can make things happen
- Bethune has a knack for setting clear, simple performance targets that everyone can understand, and then coming up with policies and incentives to drive the organization to achieve them – the true job of a turnaround CEO
- He is an **excellent communicator**. There is no doubt about where he stands and what he thinks. Employees know that he means what he says, and adopts a tough, no-nonsense style in dealing with employees.

He is not afraid to make tough decisions; he can explain the need for them and win employee acceptance of them. Bethune and other Continental executives **did a very effective job of communicating that the Go Forward plan was management's blueprint**—there were meetings with employees at virtually every site in the company to introduce the plan and explain how it addressed all of Continental's problems; **this helped get practically all employees on**

board (many of whom were ready for something good to happen to the company and were thus willing to pitch in and do their part). **Winning the cooperation of the whole Continental organization was no small feat and it certainly explains much of Bethune's success.**

The four elements of the Go Forward Plan:

- The Market Plan (Fly to Win)
- The Product Plan (Make Reliability a Reality)
- The Financial Plan (Fund the Future), and
- The People Plan (Working Together)

Bring out very well the key elements needed for a successful turnaround plan in the **phases of Surgery, Resuscitation and Nursing.**

The Plan was structured around a clearly defined broad differentiation strategy keyed to clean, safe, reliable service from well-managed hubs, convenient flight schedules and on-time arrivals, an array of amenities to make passenger travel pleasant and comfortable, and rewarding frequent flyer benefits. The primary target market was business travelers.

a) The Fly to Win market plan called for Continental to stop doing those things that were losing money or causing the company to lose money and to concentrate on Continental's market strengths.   (Surgery and Resuscitation)

b) The Fly to Win Plan entailed drastic cutbacks in Continental Lite flights and substantially revising Continental's route schedule to focus on hub-and-spoke operations rather than point-to-point routes. More flights were scheduled for new spoke locations that held promise of generating enough passenger traffic to generate a profit. (Resuscitation and Nursing)

c) The changes made in Continental's flight schedules/routes, combined with the reduced number of planes comprising the fleet, helped

   i.   position Continental in higher traffic markets,
   ii.   allow maintenance to be performed more sensibly and economically,
   iii. strengthen Continental's hub operations, and
   iv.   Improve the company's overall load factor

   all of which contributed to improving the company's financial and operating performance.

d) The marketing piece of the plan entailed launching a concerted marketing campaign to win back customers that it had lost, especially business travelers. The strategic decisions to win favor with travel agents and to court business travelers were crucial because they were willing to pay higher fares in return for good service, comfort, convenience, on-time arrivals, and accurate baggage-handling; these passengers also provided higher profit margins. (Nursing)

e) Restoration of the features of the award-winning One-Pass frequent flyer program that prior management had dismantled. (Surgery)

f) The code-sharing agreements with airline partners. (Resuscitation)

g) The "Make Reliability a Reality" feature of the plan—essential for an effective turnaround of operations. (Nursing)

h) The several initiatives to strengthen Continental's balance sheet and begin to produce a return for shareholders. (Nursing)

Question 3
Do you think the Go Forward Plan was entirely successful? On hindsight, what aspect of the Plan, if any, was wrong with the Go Forward Plan?

In large measure, there can be no second opinion about the success of the Go Forward Plan enunciated by Gordon Bethune. All the points mentioned in Question 2 are clear indicators of how successful the Plan had been.

It is only on hindsight that one can possibly see two weaknesses in the Go Forward Plan:

a) The broad differentiation strategy and the many frills that had been added to please passengers had made Continental a high-cost provider. In spite of emphasizing the need to add costs only if it adds value to the customer, the differentiation strategy adopted these techniques as against the fast-growing Low-Cost Carriers. Continental's high costs may well be something the company can get by with when times are good and passengers are willing to pay the high fares, but high costs leave the company vulnerable and unprofitable when times get tough—as they did in Fall 2001. These become clear when we analyse the Operating characteristics given in exhibit 6. The Break-even load factor had jumped from 67.4% in Sept 2000 to 78.3% in Sept 2001.

b) Continental's financial strategy (Fund the Future) placed too much emphasis on debt-financing and the use of leverage to boost the company's stock price and reward shareholders. This again is more evident in hindsight and the financial difficulties precipitated in the wake of 9/11

Question 4
Assuming you were appointed as a Consultant to Continental Airlines in the Fall of 2001, what would be your recommendations to tide over the ills of reduced passenger traffic and the Company's rapid cash drain?

At this stage, it must be evident to the participants that the crisis precipitated in the Fall of 2001 is largely due to "External viruses". The only two internal viruses could be the two points mentioned under Question 3.

The participants must be encouraged to review the data in case Exhibits 4, 5, and 6, which lay out the statistics for Continental's third quarter. The dreadful passenger load factors shown in case Exhibit 4 indicate a need for bold and drastic action—especially given the high breakeven load factors that Continental had (see case Exhibit 6). **Without cutbacks, Continental would undoubtedly have hemorrhaged red ink and experienced an unsustainable cash drain that would have propelled it into bankruptcy.** So, in a very real sense, Bethune's actions were necessary to save the company.

Another important point to be made here is that Bethune's turnaround strategy and the success he had achieved up until 9/11 was indeed more fragile than might have been suspected. Whereas the Low-Cost Carriers would have pursued a strategy and operated in a manner that was "built to last", Bethune's turnaround was built on a foundation that quickly crumbled when hit with major adversity and a sharp erosion of high-fare business travel. **High fares and high passenger load factors are essential for Continental's strategy and business to prove profitable.** This is an important point to drive home—and it comes out very clearly from a careful examination of the statistics presented in case Exhibits 1, 2, 4, 5, and 6

From every indication, the company is reeling as of November 2001, although it will probably survive because of the cash infusions provided by the federal bailout and because, at some point, business travel is likely to rebound. An economic upturn and an absence of more terrorist attacks should allow Continental to survive the cash crisis and perhaps return to profitability as soon as the second half of 2002.

Some of the recommendations that can be expected to bail out Continental as of Fall 2001 and tide over the reduced passenger traffic and the cash drain are:

a) Re-examine costs and see what low value-added expenses can temporarily be cut out—there is an urgent need to **stem the negative cash flows and protect the company's financial viability**. There may be some savings in temporarily reducing some of the frills provided to passengers.

b) Monitor traffic levels closely and move quickly to resume some of the flights that were cut in September-October 2001 when and where traffic permits. Barring further terrorists attacks, passenger traffic is likely to rebound to pre-9/11 levels by late 2002 (if not sooner), especially if the economy rebounds also (as seemed to have occurred by March 2002).

c) Look hard for opportunities to add new flights/routes. The importance of resuming flights cut earlier and adding new routes is to get grounded planes and laid-off employees back to work and **boost Continental's revenues as fast and as much as possible** (and move from negative daily cash flows to positive daily cash flows). **The best way for Continental to stem the cash drain is to sell more tickets and transport more passengers.**

d) Consider **special fare promotions** to help stimulate the return of passenger traffic. But too much discounting can lead to little if any revenue gains—and Continental needs revenue growth badly to restore profitability. Profitability and **positive cash flows at Continental are not going to come from simply cutting expenses—it is going to come from top line revenue growth.**

e) **Bethune** needs to be visible in encouraging and motivating employees. He **has to use his considerable communication skills to rally the troops to the cause of getting Continental through this temporary crisis** and giving 100% effort. What employees have to do is help watch costs and do a great job of pleasing customers and continuing to achieve good operating performance (as measured by the metric of on-time arrivals).

f) To nurture the culture and promote continued teamwork and trust, Bethune ought to **frequently praise employee efforts, provide positive reinforcement, and instill confidence** that Continental can overcome the adversities it confronts. These next 12 months, Bethune ought to repeatedly push the theme that each Continental employee is a part of what is happening at Continental, that **Continental's people are still the company, and that the Working Together Plan is alive and well despite the adversity in the marketplace.** He needs to convince

Continental employees that in no way has management wavered on its commitment to making Continental a place where people are treated with dignity and respect and are happy to come to work. He needs to continue to do the things that will keep Continental on Fortune's list of the 100 best companies to work for in America.

Suggested Answers and Analysis - Avid Technology Case

Needless to say, in a case study, we are always open to new ideas and interpretation coming from the delegates, and hence there are obviously no absolutely correct or wrong answers. The suggested answers given below are indicative of the points that are expected to be analysed by the delegates / participants during the case discussion.

Question 1
What is your assessment of Avid Technology's financial condition when David Krall took over? Are there clear indications of failing health over a period of time? Substantiate your answers with numbers from the case.

In analyzing the financial health of Avid Technology Inc, it is important to understand what the key drivers for Avid's growth were in the initial years, and what accounted for the top-line stagnation subsequently.

To put some numbers in perspective, Avid Technology grew from revenues of $1 million in 1989 to $ 407 million in 1995 – an astounding growth of 400 times (40,000% flat rate) in 7 years!!!. After that, the revenues had stagnated between $420 million and $ 480 million during the period from 1996 to 2000.

Avid's success sprung essentially from the **entrepreneurial genius** of its founders. With their strong industry backgrounds, the company's founders were able to identify the need for a better way of editing moving pictures, graphics, and sound in the creation of movie films and television programming. Avid was **an early technology mover**, using digital technology as a substitute for analog-based technology and coming up with an application that simplified and added flexibility to the jobs of media editors.

Avid was first to market with this new technology and **supported open industry standards to enhance its adoption, thus enabling the company to grow market share quickly during its early years.** In addition, the company **pursued sales opportunities in foreign markets early, generating 42% of total revenues from international markets** within the first three full fiscal years of its founding. As a result, Avid was able to achieve a bigger unit sales volume and spread research and development costs across a larger market and customer base.

In short, the phenomenal success of Avid till 1995 was based on:

- entrepreneurial creativity (**innovation**)
- capitalization on its **first mover advantage,** and
- the strategy to sell its innovative Media Composer **across the world.**

In the years after 1995, the main reason for revenue stagnation has been Avid's **inability to come up with additional innovative products** of much significance **and the market saturation** for Media Composer causing the company to peak in the mid-1990s and incur losses by the end of the decade.

The company's financial statements are shown in case Exhibits 1 and 2.

a) Sales growth following 1995 slowed, with revenues increasing only 5% to $429 million in 1996, 10% to $471 million in 1997, and 2% to $482 million in 1998. In 1999, revenues decreased for the first time in the company's history, dropping 6% to $453 million. In 2000, revenues were up about 6% to $476 million.

b) The company has lost money in 4 of the past 5 years; in the past 2 years the company has lost a total of $196 million.

c) The company's stock price had suffered, reflecting the company's poor bottom line and uncertain future prospects.

From an examination of case Exhibits 1 and 2, we can conclude that Avid's financial performance has deteriorated since 1998:

i. Given the company's losses in 4 of the past 5 years, Avid's profitability ratios are below par:

	1996	1997	1998	1999	2000
Gross profit margins of	44.3%	53.0%	60.6%	54.5%	50.8%
Operating profit margins of	(7.0)%	6.4%	10.3%	0.0%	2. 5%
Net profit margins of	(8.9)%	5.6%	(0.7)%	(30.4)%	(11.8)%

ii. In 1999, Avid recorded revenues of $452.6 million, a 6% decrease from 1998, and a net loss of $137.5 million – the company's worst performance in its 10-year history. Further, from 1998 to 1999, cash and marketable securities decreased from $111.8 million to $72.8 million; the current ratio decreased from 2:1 to 1.7:1, and long-term debt as a percentage of equity increased from 4.6% to 8.5%.

iii. The company's sales have grown at a meager 2.5% compound average rate since 1996.

iv. Avid's gross profit margin has eroded significantly since 1998, dropping from ($482.4 million in sales / $292.2 million in gross profit) to 50.8%.

v.   Cash and marketable securities have decreased 25.6% in the past two years—from $111.8 million in 1998 to $83.2 million in 2000.

vi.   The 69 days outstanding for accounts receivable in 2000 ($90 million in receivables against $476.0 million in sales), although consistent with that of 1998, appears excessive, given industry norms of 45 to 60 days.

vii.   Inventory turnover has also deteriorated from 43.5 times in 1998 ($482.4 million in sales / $11.1 million in inventory) to 22.6 times in 2000.

viii. The company's long-term debt as a percentage of equity has increased from 4.6% in 1998 ($13.3 million in long-term debt / $290.3 million in stockholders' equity) to 9.7% in 2000. This is primarily due to the excessive losses incurred during 1999 and 2000 (largely due to the amortization of the Softimage acquisition) which have placed the company in a retained earnings deficit position of $197.8 million at the end of 2000.

ix.   The company's property, plant, and equipment balance has decreased by $26.3 million from 1998 to 2000, indicating that the company is not systematically upgrading aging assets or reinvesting in the business. (An alternative explanation is that Avid has plenty of fixed assets to support current operations and near-term growth.)

x.   The company's balance sheet is, however, not alarmingly bad; the company is certainly not on the brink of bankruptcy, despite the losses and the negative retained earnings. Fortunately Avid has little long-term debt and it has almost $97 million in working capital (working capital = current assets - current liabilities). So Avid's financial condition, while weaker than one might like, is by no means desperate. But there can be no doubt that the company needs to move toward profitability and be operating in the black by 2002 if at all possible.

All these are very clear pointers to a progressively declining health of Avid Technology Inc.

Question 2
What steps taken by David Krall pertain to the Surgery phase of corporate turnaround?

As of the period till when the facts are presented in the case, **David Krall had essentially diagnosed what his predecessors had done (or undone),** and was just about completing the diagnosis and surgery phase with a few steps.

In this context, it will be appropriate to recount what the previous CEOs had done, and then see what David Krall's strategy has been.

Avid's strategy under its first two CEOs had several key components that come out clearly in the case:

a. **Pursue sales opportunities** for the company's digital technology products in the film, television, radio, and news broadcast industries
b. **Develop sales capabilities** in many locations **across the world**
c. Explore opportunities for Avid Cinema in the retail consumer market (such opportunities were expected to be modest for about five years while the market developed, but were then expect to grow rapidly)
d. Spend about **17% of revenues on R&D to** develop new products (but not much has come from this effort lately)
e. **Make acquisitions to purchase leading technology** in the form of existing products and capabilities that the company believed complemented its existing in-house technology (see case Exhibit 4 for a listing)
f. **Form alliances** with other firms to help develop new technologies
g. Grow the company's product line via **acquisitions and alliances and internal R&D**—product portfolio now includes six general categories: video and film editing products, audio products, digital news gathering systems, newsroom computer systems, graphics and special effects products, and storage systems. These products ranged widely in price and target market (and, in effect, represent different businesses).
h. Take the **lead in developing and promoting open industry standards** for digital technology. (The company released into the public domain the platform of basic digital technology it developed and applied to specific product creations.)
i. Develop stronger relationships with firms that could distribute Avid's

products to a broad base of commercial and retail customers and **reduce direct sales (in-house) activities to only key accounts** that required a significant amount of time during the sales and post-sales process.

j. **Pay more attention to the customer support function,** by expanding resources and restructuring the function to increase customer satisfaction.

In spite of these excellent strategic steps, **Avid's top line did not show any signs of increasing. What this implied obviously was that there is severe market saturation – typical of quite a few high-tech products.**

During his first year as CEO, **David Krall announced a new focus on Internet-related editing products and once again set Avid on an acquisition track.** In 2000, Avid purchased Pluto Technologies International Inc. and The Motion Factory Inc. for an aggregate $2.3 million. Pluto Technologies specialized in storage and networking products for the news broadcast industry, and The Motion Factory specialized in interactive games for the web. These were Avid's first acquisitions since its questionable 1998 acquisition of Softimage. **Krall also helped spearhead an alliance with Intel and Microsoft** to develop products for creating interactive digital television.

Thus it is evident that Krall's initial steps were focused on **sustaining the current revenue levels** through appropriate acquisitions, since Avid was clearly facing a market that had adopted the technology quickly and new avenues to increase sales were required. David Krall's surgery steps were mainly on the cash flow front and profitability front.

Krall finished his first year with Avid showing some promise of a turnaround. Avid's 2000 revenues were up 5% from 1999, and, the company's net loss of $56 million was significantly less than the $137 million loss in 1999.

Question 3
Discuss and evaluate the Blood Transfusion techniques used by Avid management before and under David Krall. In your opinion, was the Softimage acquisition the right treatment for Avid?

Whether Blood Transfusion was an appropriate treatment or not, to cure the illness Avid was suffering from since 1996 is a difficult question to answer. But there are some strong clues scattered throughout the case, despite the lack of detailed data about individual products and businesses that Avid got into through acquisitions and alliances (Case exhibit 4 gives the specific details of the significant acquisitions carried out by Avid):

a) Avid's sales revenues had been fairly flat for 4 years despite the series of acquisitions that have been made in this interval. So far, the acquired technologies and products do not seem to have produced much top line growth (we don't know/can't tell, however, if they have kept sales revenues from dropping perhaps sharply, though—which could be the case if sales of the Media Composer are weakening because of market saturation).

b) The Avid Cinema product apparently has long-term potential in the retail consumer market, but modest short-term potential.

c) Softimage does not appear to be a contributor at this point (except for the negative of increasing depreciation charges for goodwill incurred in the acquisition price). Avid paid a hefty $248 million to acquire a company with $38 million in revenues

d) The case indicates that Digidesign under Krall's leadership was a solid growth and profit performer.

e) With a compound average growth rate in revenues of only 2.5% since 1996, it is hard to get excited about the revenue potential of the company's current product line and business portfolio that have come through largely because of blood transfusion.

Talking of the major acquisition in 1998 (Softimage at a price of $248 million), information in the case indicates that Softimage has some excellent 3D and animation software products (and one would surmise there are probably more upgrades or complementary products in the Softimage pipeline). What stands out here is that this was a major acquisition for Avid. The company paid $248 million to acquire Softimage, an amount equal to **6.7x Softimage's revenues** (we do not know if Softimage was profitable at the time of its acquisition, but one suspects not). For this acquisition to come close to paying off for Avid, Avid will have to grow sales of Softimage products by 3-4 times (to over $100 million) and at the same time realize attractive profit margins; **Softimage would have to add $25 million to Avid's bottom line for the company to realize just a 10% return on its acquisition price of $248 million**—and this would entail a 10-year payback of the acquisition price!

There is no solid indication from the information provided in the case that Softimage has this kind of potential. If Softimage pays off for Avid shareholders, it will have to be down the road—Avid appears to have bought "potential" not current performance.

What Softimage may bring to the table for Avid is a more complete line of products for film producers, to complement Avid's once hot Media Composer and its other film and media digital technology products. **Avid needs a continuing stream of new products just to keep its revenues in the $400-$500 million range** (where they have been for the last 5 years)—Avid's businesses are all positioned in product markets that apparently have short product-life cycles and a fairly limited customer base (except for Avid Cinema which is said to have potential in the retail consumer market at some point).

Considering all these points, past acquisitions as well as Softimage have been the appropriate strategies for Avid, given the product-market cycles.

Question 4
As a turnaround consultant to Avid Technology, what recommendations will you make to David Krall?

Considering the detailed analysis given above with respect to the types of illnesses Avid Technology has been afflicted by, the best lines of action towards Resuscitation and Nursing of Avid that David Krall should take are as follows:

a) Push hard for internal cost reduction. Avid's revenue base is not high enough to support the present level of operating expenses.

b) Try to accelerate new product introductions (ideally with minimal additional R&D expenditures). Avid needs more revenue-generating products—higher revenues, along with cuts in operating expenses, are the key to becoming profitable in late 2001 or 2002, and beyond.

c) Consider new acquisitions to expand the company's product offerings to existing customers. We think any new acquisitions should entail products which can be marketed to Avid's present customer base at minimal incremental cost (so as to leverage the company's present sales and marketing capabilities). Acquisitions with good strategic and resource fits would seem far superior to those that launch Avid in altogether new market arenas.

d) Go slow on committing new resources to developing the retail market for Avid Cinema—any such effort could be relatively expensive, stretch Avid's resources too thinly, and not yield much in the way of additional revenue for 3-5 years. Avid needs to concentrate the available resources on near-term market opportunities and restore profitability as quickly as it can.

www.ingramcontent.com/pod-product-compliance
Lightning Source LLC
Chambersburg PA
CBHW070724220326
41598CB00024BA/3290